Space, Stars, and Quasars

Ron Benson

Lynn Bryan

Kim Newlove

Charolette Player

Liz Stenson

CONSULTANTS

Susan Elliott

Diane Lomond

Ken MacInnis

Elizabeth Parchment

Prentice Hall Ginn Canada
Scarborough, Ontario

26

Contents

Bibliography

🎧 Selections with this symbol are available on audio.

✏️ This symbol indicates student writing.

🍁 Canadian selections are marked with this symbol.

Earth and Moon

The First

by Lilian Moore

Moon,
remember
how men left their
planet
in streams of
flame,
rode weightless
in the skies
till you pulled
them down,
and then
in the blinding sunlight
how the first shadow
of an
Earthling
lay
on your
bleak dust?

Orbiter 5 Shows How Earth Looks from the Moon

by May Swenson

There's a woman in the earth, sitting on her heels. You see her from the back, in three-quarter profile. She has a flowing pigtail. She's holding something

in her right hand—some holy jug. Her left arm is thinner, in a gesture like a dancer. She's the Indian Ocean. Asia is light swirling up out of her vessel. Her pigtail points to Europe and her dancer's arm is the Suez Canal. She is a woman in a square kimono,

bare feet tucked beneath the tip of Africa. Her tail of long hair is the Arabian Peninsula.

A woman in the earth.

A man in the moon.

Spacewalk

by Doug Murray
Illustrated by Russ Willms

Five . . . Four . . . All systems on internal . . .

Tommy squirmed against the straps holding him. They were so *tight!* He felt trapped, something he'd always hated. Maybe if he shifted his body, twisted to the left a little—maybe then the straps would loosen just the least little bit . . .

Three . . . Two . . . Main engine ignition sequence started . . .

Tommy felt the straps give slightly. Good! He shifted back the other way, trying to gain a little leverage.

One . . . Solid boosters fire . . .

The world exploded in sound! Tommy felt himself forced down into his cushions, his whole body suddenly weighing a tonne. He tried to take a deep breath—but he couldn't even get enough air into his lungs to cry out.

Tommy lay quietly on the cushions. He was miserable and he had to work just to breathe. His head was so heavy he couldn't even lift it. The roaring sound filled his head, hurt his ears. If only it would stop!

Tommy squeezed his eyes shut, hoping that someone would make things right again. He saw black with little glittery stars slowly filling his vision. It was getting worse, he was getting heavier and heavier, the sound louder and louder . . .

Then it stopped.

"Through the sound barrier. Engines nominal at 110 percent," said Jack Dodds, the mission pilot.

"Roger." Commander Stacy Mayberry glanced back into the cabin, neck aching as she set her muscles against the three Gs still pressing against her. "Everyone OK back there? How's Tommy doing?"

"Tommy's doing fine, Skipper! Says he wants to know when these

Gs drop off," said Mission Specialist Mike Mize.

"So do we all!" added Alice Norton, the second Mission Specialist on the flight.

Mayberry turned her head back toward the control board. "Clock says another two minutes. Just hold on!"

Tommy was breathing shallowly, almost panting. It felt as though two or three other Tommys were lying right on his chest. He'd been through all this in preflight training, but he still didn't like it. The truth was, nobody did.

Mayberry glanced at the mission clock, then placed her hands carefully on the manual overrides. "Thirty seconds! Jack, get ready on those manuals!"

"Right, Skipper!"

"Five . . . Four . . . Three . . . Two . . . Engine cutoff . . . Now!"

Tommy's body suddenly stopped aching. He blinked, his vision clearing. Opening his eyes wide, he tried to see all around him at once. He felt so different, like . . .

He was falling! Instinctively, he fought against the straps still holding him in place. He twisted his legs trying desperately to get free . . .

"All right, everyone. We're in stable orbit." Mayberry grinned as she looked at the green faces on the crew deck. "And we're weightless."

"Tell me about it!" groaned Alice.

"Don't tell *me*—tell my stomach!" said Mike.

Alice smiled encouragingly at Tommy. "Hang in there. You've been through all this in training—this is supposed to be the payoff, remember?"

Tommy gave the Mission Specialist a reproachful look as she reached over and gave his shoulder a friendly pat.

Mayberry loosened her safety straps, chuckling as she pulled out one of the mission books. "Just stay strapped in for a few minutes until you get the feel of it. Jack, after we run the checklist, pass out antinausea pills to anyone who feels the need."

"You got it, Skipper!"

Mayberry's grin grew wider. "And anybody who has an 'accident' waiting for those pills has to clean it up!"

"Thanks a lot, Commander!"

"What a heart!"

Tommy just lay there. He still felt as though he were falling, but he didn't seem to be getting closer to the ground. He swallowed carefully and blinked his eyes. He couldn't tell which way was down. Something was very strange!

He squirmed against the straps, but there was no give at all now. Sighing deeply, he relaxed and began to look around. He knew now that he wasn't falling and he was *definitely* not going to get sick. He'd be sure to get in trouble for that!

Time passed. The straps were no longer necessary, and Tommy soon found that weightlessness was fun! Sure, he made a few mistakes at first, but he had a good teacher, and by the third day, he felt almost normal again.

"OK, Tommy," Alice said one morning. "Let's see you get across the afterdeck!"

Tommy looked at her smiling face on the other side of the deck and, blinking once, he calculated distances in his head. Then he pushed off with his legs, a little too hard, his eyes widening as the deck rushed toward him. He was going *way* too fast! Tommy twisted his body frantically, trying to get his feet under him. He remembered how easy this sort of thing had always been on Earth and wondered if he'd ever get the trick of it in this new place. He thumped into the aft wall, *whuffing* as all the breath was knocked out of him.

"Tommy!" Alice pulled herself to his side, careful not to move away from the safety lines. "Tommy! Are you all right?"

Tommy shook his head hard, almost sneezing—and found himself drifting away from the floor. He realized what had happened and turned his body, stretching out to reach the safety lines on the wall. But they were too far away.

Alice was there, pulling him back to the wall until he got a good grip. He locked onto one of the safety lines, and she clipped another onto his harness. "Anything hurt?" Alice turned him over, checking his limbs, massaging his back. He stretched out, basking in the attention.

"Is he OK, Alice?" Mike Mize floated into the afterdeck, one hand holding a clipboard. "Tommy's supposed to help us with another experiment this afternoon."

Alice smiled, giving Tommy an affectionate hug. "He'll be ready. Won't you, Tommy?"

Tommy looked at the floating man and sighed, blinking his eyes. Mike was OK, but always in a hurry—and so loud!

Mike laughed. "Doesn't talk much, does he?"

"Does it matter?" Alice laughed back.

That afternoon the whole crew assembled in the afterdeck to watch the experiment. Tommy was at one end of the deck next to Alice, his safety harness clipped to one of the deck lines.

"All right, folks," Alice said, motioning to Mike that she was ready, "let's give it a try."

Mike's hand disappeared into one of the lockers mounted on the wall. "As you know," he began, "one of the things we've been looking at to relieve the boredom of long-term interplanetary missions is the introduction of pets into the spacecraft environment."

Alice gave Tommy a quick scratch behind the ears, and he instantly rewarded her with a purr. "One of the reasons we haven't brought any of the higher animals—cats, dogs, whatever—," she continued, "was because of the problem of weightlessness. Experts believed that animals just couldn't cope with that feeling of constant falling."

She picked Tommy up, releasing his collar from the safety line. "Tommy is going to show that they're wrong—aren't you, boy?" He purred again, louder this time. "And to prove it . . ." She gestured to Mike, who produced a catnip mouse. Moving with exaggerated care, he released it in the middle of the room, where it hung, drifting and motionless.

"Now, Tommy!" But Tommy had already smelled the catnip, its aroma spread through the cabin by the air-circulating system. He settled himself against the rear wall, his claws hooked tightly into the cloth of the safety straps. Then, blinking his eyes, he pushed off toward the mouse—gently, so gently.

"Note his control of the leap," Alice said quietly as Tommy moved toward the centre of the room. "Now, any second . . ."

Tommy twisted his rear right leg, forcing his body to swing around, even as his mouth closed—gently, always gently—on the little mouse.

"Note how he turns, using only slight muscular effort . . ."

Holding the mouse in his teeth, Tommy finished his turn, now twisting his left front leg to stop his tumble. He stayed in position, watching the wall grow in front of him until . . .

"Now, as he reaches the wall . . ."

He let his four legs hit together, grabbing the nearest strap with his claws and holding on as he rebounded slightly.

Alice's smile lit up the whole room. "Did you see that? And he's only had three days to practise!"

Commander Mayberry shook her head in wonder. "This is my eighth flight, and *I* can't do it that smoothly!"

Alice worked her way over to Tommy. "Cats are the answer," she said reaching into her coverall for a piece of cheese. Tommy accepted it politely from her hand. "Cats can adapt to conditions here—and cats will help make the long planetary missions more bearable to human astronauts."

Mayberry leaned forward, petting Tommy gently. "Works for me!"

Tommy began purring again as he savored the piece of cheese. It worked for him, too!

ABOUT THE AUTHOR   DOUG MURRAY

Doug Murray began his career by writing movie articles and previews for a variety of journals. He eventually branched out to write award-winning comic books, and then began publishing short stories and novels. Doug currently lives in Deltona, Florida, where he continues to write. He based his story "Spacewalk" upon the cat in the photograph.

The Astronaut Files

The Canadian Astronaut Program was established in 1983 after the United States invited Canada to fly an astronaut on board a space shuttle mission. The first six astronauts were chosen in December, 1983. In 1992, more astronauts were chosen, and since then three have resigned. So, today, Canada has seven astronauts.

What do astronauts actually do in the space shuttle? Pilot astronauts are in charge of flight control and the overall command of the shuttle. Canadian astronauts can be either Payload or Mission Specialists. Payload Specialists conduct experiments on board. They receive intensive scientific training as well as basic training in the operating systems of the orbiter, the part of the space shuttle that actually enters space. Mission Specialist astronauts may also do experiments. However, their main responsibility is to operate orbiter systems including the Canadarm, which is often used to place and retrieve payloads in orbit. Mission Specialists are also trained for Extra-Vehicular Activity (EVA), or spacewalk. They repair spacecraft and perform other operations in the orbiter cargo bay.

Now, meet Canada's astronauts of today. Get the facts about them, the secrets of their success, and their messages to students everywhere.

Steven Glenwood MacLean

Date and Place of Birth: December 14, 1954; Ottawa, Ontario

Higher Education: Bachelor of Science, Honours Physics; Doctorate in Physics

Astronaut Category: Payload Specialist

Training and Missions: selected in 1983; Payload Specialist on space shuttle *Columbia* mission, October 22–November 1, 1992; has also done research experiments testing a Canadian space vision system for the Canadarm and other robots

Interests: hiking, especially in the mountains; canoeing; gymnastics; flying

Facts Plus: member of National Gymnastics Team 1976–1977

Secret of Success: "Curiosity and intrigue coupled with a sense for fun and adventure."

Message: "Multimedia technology bombards us with so much data that it can be overwhelming and even frightening. But within this flood of data are pockets of information that are fascinating. If you develop this fascination into a passion, the passion turns to adventure, and the fear becomes a shadow."

Marc Garneau

Date and Place of Birth: February 23, 1949; Quebec City, Quebec

Higher Education: Bachelor of Science in Engineering Physics; Doctorate in Electrical Engineering

Astronaut Category: Mission Specialist

Training and Missions: selected in 1983; flew as Payload Specialist on space shuttle *Challenger,* October 5–13, 1984; flew as Mission Specialist on space shuttle *Endeavor,* May 19–May 29, 1996; first non-American to assume the duties of CAPCOM (Capsule Communicator), providing the only direct voice-link between Mission Control and the astronauts in the space shuttle

Interests: flying; scuba diving; squash; tennis; home repairs

Facts Plus: in 1969 and again in 1970, sailed across the Atlantic Ocean on an eighteen-metre yawl with twelve other crew

Secret of Success: "Although I haven't always followed my own advice and I am still very far from being the wise person I seek to become, I have found it helpful not to take myself too seriously. We all experience failure and embarrassment in our lives and a sense of humor can really keep you going."

Message: "Believe in yourself and dare to stretch ten percent beyond what you believe is your limit. You will be surprised, and once you have surpassed your own expectations, you won't ever settle for less than your best."

Chris A. Hadfield

Date and Place of Birth: August 29, 1959; Sarnia, Ontario

Higher Education: Honours Bachelor of Mechanical Engineering; US Air Force Test Pilot School; Masters of Aviation Systems

Astronaut Category: Mission Specialist

Training and Missions: selected by Canadian Space Agency in June, 1992; flew on space shuttle *Atlantis,* November 12–20, 1995; first Canadian to fly as a Mission Specialist, to board the Russian space station *Mir*, and to operate the Canadarm in space; Chief Astronaut for the CSA; Chief CAPCOM for NASA

Interests: downhill and water skiing; squash; scuba diving; horseback riding; sailing; writing; singing; playing the guitar; men's and co-ed volleyball leagues; coaching junior soccer

Facts Plus: has flown over two thousand hours in more than fifty different aircraft types

Secret of Success: "Find something you like to do, and then work at it until you do it better than anyone else."

Message: "Whenever you are faced with a decision of what to do next, chose a path that looks interesting and fun, and that leads in the direction of your long-term goals."

Robert Brent Thirsk

Date and Place of Birth: August 17, 1953; New Westminster, British Columbia

Higher Education: Bachelor of Science in Mechanical Engineering; Master of Science in Mechanical Engineering; Doctorate of Medicine

Astronaut Category: Payload Specialist

Training and Missions: selected for astronaut team in December, 1983; back-up specialist for Marc Garneau for the October 1984 mission; Chief Astronaut, 1993 and 1994; on space shuttle *Columbia* mission to Spacelab June 20–July 7, 1996—one of the longest missions in the history of NASA's shuttle flights

Interests: flying; playing squash; playing the piano

Facts Plus: has helped design an experimental "anti-gravity suit" that may help astronauts re-adapt more easily to life on Earth

Secret of Success: "I have often dreamed of doing incredible things. My parents and teachers taught me that, with planning and hard work, dreams sometimes become reality. One of my dreams was to be an astronaut."

Message: "Anything worth doing is worth doing well."

Bjarni Tryggvason

Date and Place of Birth: September 21, 1945; Reykjavik, Iceland

Higher Education: Bachelor of Applied Science in Engineering Physics; postgraduate work in engineering

Astronaut Category: Payload Specialist

Training and Missions: selected for astronaut team in December, 1983; back-up Payload Specialist to Steve MacLean for space shuttle mission in October, 1992; co-investigator of space vision experiment for this mission; selected as Payload Specialist for shuttle flight launched on August 7, 1997

Interests: flying; aerobatic flying; skiing; scuba and sky diving

Facts Plus: supervises undergraduate and graduate student projects at several universities across Canada

Secret of Success: "Well-defined goals and perseverance."

Message: "Understand and be true to yourself."

DaFydd Rhys Williams

Date and Place of Birth: May 16, 1954; Saskatoon, Saskatchewan

Higher Education: Bachelor of Science in Biology; Master of Science; Doctorate in Medicine, and Master of Surgery

Astronaut Category: Mission Specialist

Training and Missions: selected for astronaut team June, 1992; learned to fly as part of astronaut training; manager of the Missions and Space Medicine Group within the astronaut program; assigned as one of crew members on space shuttle *Columbia* mission scheduled for March, 1998

Interests: flying; scuba diving; hiking; sailing; kayaking; canoeing; downhill and cross-country skiing

Facts Plus: formerly a professional scuba diving instructor; a certified Newtsuit (hard diving suit) pilot

Secret of Success: "I believe that my success may be attributed to hard work, perseverance, and the tremendous support from my wife, my family, colleagues, and friends. Without their encouragement, I am not sure that I would have had the fortitude to persist in my activities over the years."

Message: "Have the courage to believe in yourself while striving for excellence in achieving personal goals; these are both important attributes that will help you in fulfilling your dreams."

Julie Payette

Date and Place of Birth: October 20, 1963; Montreal, Quebec

Higher Education: International Baccalaureate; Bachelor of Engineering; Master of Applied Science

Astronaut Category: astronaut; in training to be Mission Specialist

Training and Missions: selected for astronaut program in July, 1992; learned to fly and parachute as part of first-year general astronaut training; microgravity science experiments; military jet training; deep-sea diving-suit training program; began Mission Specialist training August 12, 1996, to qualify for future shuttle assignments

Interests: playing piano; singing in choir and solo soprano; competing in triathlons (biking, running, swimming); skiing; racquet sports; scuba diving

Facts Plus: fluent in French and English; conversational in Spanish, Italian, German, and Russian

Secret of Success: "There is no miracle recipe or magic road to follow but one of the keys is to maintain a positive attitude and to be true to oneself."

Message: "The important thing is to take control of one's life and not to be discouraged when times are difficult, and above all, to follow one's dreams."

YOU ASKED ABOUT SPACE

by the editors of OWL Magazine
Illustrated by Phillippe Germaine

Why is space so cold?

Here on Earth, a layer of gases called the atmosphere surrounds the planet. Earth's atmosphere acts like a big blanket to hold in air and heat from the sun. Without these gases, we'd all be frozen solid! Out in space, there are lots of stars giving off heat, as our sun does, but there is no atmosphere to hold in the heat. In fact, there are very few atoms of any kind of gas floating around. A whole lot of nothing doesn't trap very much heat. The result? Brrrrrr!

Are there any space aliens?

So far, scientists haven't found any proof that there is life beyond Earth. But they're still looking! Since 1960, researchers have made more than fifty searches for radio signals coming from space. In 1992, a NASA program called the Search for Extraterrestrial Intelligence joined the investigation. Radio telescopes linked with computers now search a much larger area of space than ever before. NASA hasn't found anything. It might mean there aren't any space aliens—or that we haven't found them yet!

ow do astronauts drink in space?

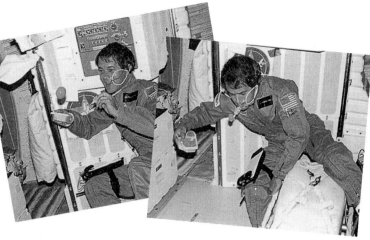

Space is a great place to play with your food because there's much less gravity on a space shuttle orbiting Earth than there is on the planet itself. In this "microgravity," an astronaut can twirl carrot sticks or send a half-peeled banana spinning with its peel sticking out like propeller blades! Drinking orange juice the space-age way is fun too. Astronaut Joe Allen (see photos) squeezes a bit of juice from a package. Because of the total lack of gravity, it simply floats as a sphere. After Joe inserts his straw, he sucks it up until the sphere gets smaller and the juice is gone!

I s there such a thing as stardust?

Yes! When a star explodes, pieces of it blast into space. Some of this "stardust" is as small as Earth dust; some of it is the size of boulders. The stardust floats around until it's sucked into another star or enough of it gathers together to form a new planet. If you'd like to see some stardust for yourself, look under your bed. Chances are there's some stardust in among the other bits of dust you'll find there, because Earth still picks up more than a thousand tonnes of stardust a day as it travels through space!

W hy shouldn't you look at a solar eclipse?

Staring at the sun is a no-no but looking at a solar eclipse is just plain dangerous. Why? When sun shines in your face, your eyes naturally shut to avoid the sun's harmful rays. During a solar eclipse the moon moves in front of the sun, blocking the sun's visible rays, and daylight darkens. Bit by bit, the sun gets hidden behind the moon until only a thin wedge of sunlight is visible around the moon. Because the sun can no longer shine, your eyes won't shut to protect you. Instead, they'll stay wide open. This bit of sunlight may seem harmless, but looking straight at

the sun—for even a few seconds!—can damage your eyes forever. Once the sun is completely hidden behind the moon and the eclipse is "total," it's okay to have a look. But at any other time don't peek—it could be the last thing you ever see.

Can Earthlings live in space?

You could live on Mars someday, as long as scientists can figure out how to keep you happy and healthy in space! Research is going on—in orbit and on the ground—to find out exactly what's needed for Earthlings to live in space. So far they know that your muscles will shrink because of all the "floating around" so you'll need lots of exercise to stay physically fit. You can't order pizza up into space so you'll need hydroponics, or soil-free gardens, to grow your food. Astronauts say that pictures of your friends and family are important to have because living in space could get pretty lonely. There is one far-out fact that's for sure: living in space will be out of this world!

Why do astronauts train in the Vomit Comet?

To train for the "floating feeling" of space, astronauts ride the KC-135—also known as the Vomit Comet. This special airplane blasts astronauts straight up into the air and then dives almost straight down. Ugg! At the very top of the plane's arc, just before it heads downward, astronauts-in-training feel like they've said "goodbye" to gravity! They begin to "free fall," which gives them the feeling of being weightless. This floating feeling lasts for only twenty-five seconds, but that's too long for some stomachs-in-training to handle! Actors and filmmakers for the movie *Apollo 13* took the KC-135 on seventeen flights—that's over 609 zero gravity arcs!

ow long does it take to get to space?

A space shuttle could blast you into space at an eyeball-popping speed of 28 000 km/h. That's about ten times faster than a Concorde jet! The trip into space would take less than a minute, and on your way up you'd pass through Earth's atmosphere. You'd tear past clouds in the troposphere, streak by jets in the stratosphere, and motor by weather balloons in the mesosphere. At around one hundred kilometres above Earth, you'd be in the middle of the thermosphere and at the beginning of what we call "space." By putting your shuttle's pedal to the metal, you could cruise into orbit. To head back home, you'd just cut the juice, glide in, and let gravity pull you back down. What a trip!

f there's no air in space, what is there?

Higher than about thirty-two kilometres above the ground, there's hardly any air, and far out in space there isn't any at all. That's why it's called space—it's almost completely empty. Special instruments on spacecraft have found a few specks of dust, as well as some atoms thrown off the sun by solar flares and some fast-moving particles called cosmic rays. But there are so few of these that you wouldn't notice them if you were right out there in space with them. In fact, all you would see is darkness—and thousands of stars.

Why do people float in outer space?

If you have ever bounced on a trampoline, or felt a sinking feeling in your stomach when flying in an airplane during turbulence, you have some idea of what it feels like to be floating in outer space. At the highest point of your bounce, you get a strange feeling of weightlessness, as if you are floating.

Rocketships that carry astronauts into space work like a trampoline. They are powerful enough to keep you travelling at a speed that escapes the force of the Earth's gravity. Thus the astronauts, and everything else not anchored down in the ship, "floats" around. How fast a spaceship must be going for its astronauts to escape from the Earth's gravity and feel weightless is determined by how far out the craft is in space— and thus how far it is from the effect of the Earth's pull. If you take off from other planets or the moon, which also have gravity that pulls things toward them, your spaceship has to go fast enough to counteract their gravitational pull also.

There is a mid-point between Earth and the moon where neither's gravity affects the spaceship, so even if the craft were stopped, the astronauts would still feel weightless. It's only when the rocket's engines are fired that the astronauts are pushed back against their chairs, just as you are when your plane takes off.

What is the moon made of?

When the astronauts travelled to the moon, they gathered rocks and dirt from the surface and brought the samples back to Earth in special boxes. Scientists who have studied this material say that the moon is made mostly of material similar to basalt, the most common type of rock we have on Earth. But the basalt on the moon has been mostly smashed into gravel-like rubble by meteorites crashing into the moon for millions of years.

Far-out Jobs

by Nancy Finton and Laura Allen
Illustrated by Margot Thompson

Tracking African elephants, spying on top-secret places . . . What could handle these tough jobs— even from kilometres away? Read on, and see what weird work satellites are getting these days.

Getting on Track

What's the best way to follow an elephant through a thick forest? Use a satellite!

"We knew almost nothing about African forest elephants," says scientist Fred Koontz. So his team snuck up on three of the huge animals. They shot them with darts full of sleeping medicine. Then they buckled on elephant-sized collars, complete with radio transmitters that could send signals to a satellite.

For the next two years, Fred could find his elephant family anywhere in their African forest—just by turning on his computer at the Bronx Zoo in New York!

"That taught us the size of the elephants' *range*—the places they go for food and water," Fred says. "And, we learned they like lowlands and rivers, but they stay away from human villages." Scientists can use this information to protect the kinds of places where elephants live.

In the meantime, Fred and his elephants are out of touch. "The batteries in their collars went dead," Fred told us. "It's like they went off the air. But we're planning to use satellites to track other animals, like sharks."

Watching over Earth

Blasting off into space gives us a good look at our planet. Satellites help scientists check out our environment—and see just how bad the problems are.

Take the pictures below, for example. Scientists are worried that Earth is slowly losing its layer of ozone. (That's a gas that protects us against harmful rays from the sun.) So they use satellite information to keep track of ozone levels.

The problem is really bad above the South Pole, where these pictures were taken. Red and yellow mean lots of ozone. Blue and green mean normal

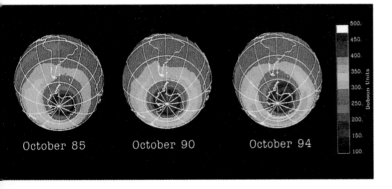

October 85   October 90   October 94

levels. But purple is bad news: It means the ozone layer is very thin. (Dark purple is the worst.)

Can you see how levels of ozone changed between 1985 and 1994? These satellite pictures show that there's a serious problem. Scientists hope the pictures can convince people to do something about the problem—before it's too late!

Frozen Science

Temperatures in the Arctic may fall below -40°C. But thousands of kids will join an Arctic expedition—and they won't even feel a chill. Why? They'll be taking part through a satellite connection! Here's how:

Four men, two women, and thirty-three dogs will journey to the North Pole for real. They'll travel by dog sled over the ice that covers the Arctic Ocean. They hope to cover more than 3200 km before the ice breaks up in the spring.

But making it across is not the team's only goal. With computers and a satellite connection, they'll teach kids about the Arctic environment. The kids will get updates on the team's progress. And, they'll get the results of environmental tests, like one for acid rain.

"People pollute the air and water all over the world," says team member Julie Hanson. "Because of winds and ocean currents, a lot of that pollution ends up in the Arctic. We want people to know that what we do down here affects life up there."

Seeing-eye Satellite

Imagine you're a blind person in a strange town. You've got a craving for an ice-cream cone. How could you tell which building is the ice-cream shop? With a new invention, you could use satellite signals!

Here's how it works: Your backpack holds an antenna and a computer. The antenna picks up signals from two or more satellites. The computer uses the signals to figure out where you are.

The computer also holds a map of the town that lists important buildings (like ice-cream shops). As you walk by each building, a computer voice says "library" or "school" or "ice-cream shop."

To steer you in the right direction, the computer adjusts the voice so it sounds like it's coming from the building. That means the sound gets louder as you get closer. Not only that, but if the building is to your left, the voice is louder in your left ear. That tells you to turn left!

Spy in the Sky

Satellites can snoop in top-secret places—they never have to sneak across borders, or climb over fences. So governments use spy satellites to check on other countries. They spy on armies, weapon factories, and lots more.

How much of a "close-up shot" can satellite cameras snap? That depends on two things:

- Height of flight: The highest satellites soar 35 000 km above Earth. But spy satellites stay just a few hundred kilometres off the planet, for a closer look.
- Powerful sight: Spy satellites carry the world's most powerful cameras. The cameras can either snap the big picture, or zoom in close for a detailed view.

All About Orbits

What's the most attractive thing about Earth? Its gravity! All day, every day, gravity pulls you "down to Earth."

Not even satellites can resist gravity's pull. In fact, they'd be lost without it—lost in outer space.

Ready to see how satellites get—and stay—in orbit? Get moving with these "out-of-this-world" experiments!

Swinging Satellites

Think: What keeps a satellite in orbit?

Get It Together
- **paper or plastic cup**
- **1-m piece of string**
- **masking tape**
- **penny**

1. Tape a piece of string to a cup.

2. Place a penny in the cup.

3. Hold the string about 25 cm from the cup. Swing the cup in a circle. What happens to the penny?

The penny and cup are a model of a satellite orbiting Earth. The penny is the satellite. Your hand is Earth. The string and cup stand for Earth's gravity.

4. Hold the string at the very end and swing the cup again. When does the cup take longer to make a circle—when the string is longer or shorter?

5. Make sure your area is clear. Swing your cup a couple of turns, then let go. What happens to the cup and penny?

Wrap Up: In your model, how is the penny like a satellite? How are the string and cup like gravity? How is your hand like Earth?

Based on your model, which do you think takes less time to orbit Earth—satellites close to or far away from Earth?

What would happen to a satellite if gravity suddenly stopped? (Hint: What happened when you let go of the string?)

Bonus: What would happen if you replaced the penny with a half cup of water? Go outside and experiment to find out.

Bull's-Eye!

Think: What keeps a satellite moving in a curve?

Get It Together

- **long, clear area (A hallway or playground works well.)**
- **masking tape**
- **beanbag (Or, use another non-rolling object, like crumpled paper or a penny.)**
- **measuring tape**
- **recording sheets**

1. Use masking tape to make an "X" on the floor.

2. Hold the beanbag over the "X" and drop it. What happens?

3. Stand about 5 m away from the "X." Hold the beanbag in your right hand, about waist high. Keep your arm against your side.

4. Walk toward the "X." As you pass the "X," drop the beanbag right above it. (Hint: Don't slow down or stop!) What happens?

When you walk, you give your beanbag *kinetic energy*—or energy of motion. When you let go, the energy keeps your beanbag moving forward. But at the same time, gravity pulls it down toward Earth. The result? The beanbag moves in a curved path. (See diagram.)

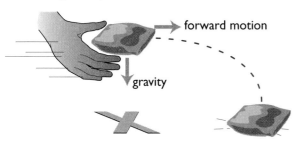

forward motion

gravity

5. Measure how far the beanbag is from the "X." Record the distance.

6. Repeat steps 3–5 twice more. (Hint: Try to walk at the same speed each time.)

7. Compare the three distances you recorded. Cross out the high and low ones.

8. Repeat steps 3–7, but this time jog instead of walk.

Wrap Up: Like your beanbag, satellites also follow a curved path. Why? A satellite is launched with a lot of energy. That energy keeps the satellite moving forward. But gravity keeps the satellite attracted to Earth. The satellite's forward motion and gravity balance each other and the satellite follows a curved path— *around* Earth. What do you think would happen to a satellite if it lost its forward motion?

When did you give your beanbag more forward motion—when you walked or jogged? Which made it travel farther? How could your beanbag be launched into orbit around the Earth?

Bonus: What would happen if you repeated this experiment while holding the beanbag at shoulder height? Experiment to find out.

Launch into Orbit

Think: A satellite has to blast off at just the right speed to get into orbit. Too slow, and it falls to Earth and crashes. Too fast, and it shoots into outer space. How would you control a satellite's orbit?

Get It Together

- **ruler with a groove down the middle (Or, tape two regular rulers in a "V" shape, as shown.)**
- **marble**
- **modelling clay**
- **desk**
- **masking tape**
- **measuring tape**
- **recording sheet**

1. Make a launch pad: Hold a ruler on a table at about a 45° angle. (That's the angle halfway between vertical and horizontal.) Secure it with modelling clay 5 cm from the table's edge. (Or, support the ruler with books or have a partner hold it.)

2. Tape an "X" on the floor about 40 cm from the table. The "X" stands for orbit. Beyond it is outer space. Before it is Earth.

3. Pick a "launch number"— a starting place on the ruler for your "satellite" (a marble). Write the number on your lab sheet.

4. Put the marble on the launch number and let go. Have a partner watch where it lands.

5. Measure and record the distance it landed from the table. (That's where it first lands, not where it rolls!)

6. Test your marble satellite at different launch numbers until it lands on the "X" three times in a row.

Wrap Up: How does the length of the launch (where you put the marble) affect where it lands? Which gives your marble satellite more energy—a long or short launch? What happens to a marble satellite that's launched with too much energy? Too little? What about real satellites?

Bonus: Does the weight of the marble affect where it lands? Design an experiment to test your predictions.

Where Do We Go from Here?

by Buzz Aldrin
Illustrated by Dave McKay

Buzz Aldrin is an American astronaut. He was the second human on the moon, and is also an expert on space systems. Here is his plan for exploring and utilizing outer space between now and the year 2020.

1998 to 2002
The fly-back booster

Aldrin urges aerospace companies and the government to move forward with existing plans for an easy-to-maintain, reusable rocket made from off-the-shelf technology that would be a cheap, dependable way to carry loads into space.

FOLD-OUT WINGS:
After the second stage is launched, the booster extends its main wings and is guided by remote control to land like a plane.

FUEL:
Liquid oxygen and kerosene power the booster's rocket engines.

JET ENGINE:
Like those used on airplanes, it propels the booster back to the launch site.

TWIN ENGINES:
Proven engines, such as RD-170s used on some Russian rockets, could power the booster.

SPACE STATION:
"We already have a space station. It's called Mir," says Aldrin. He supports refurbishing and expanding the existing Russian station with U. S. equipment to create an international orbiting base.

SECOND STAGE

SECOND STAGE:
When the booster runs out of fuel, the second stage detaches. With its own fuel, it puts satellites in orbit or takes people to space stations. This manned second stage would be smaller than the shuttle.

2005 to 2010

Back to the moon

Fly-back boosters are a key part of Aldrin's heavy lift rocket, which would send people and supplies to a future moon base. Mining operations at the base would supply space stations, spacecraft, and even the Earth with fuel. The moon's most valuable product probably will be a form of helium needed to produce clean fusion power. Rare on Earth, it is plentiful on the lunar surface.

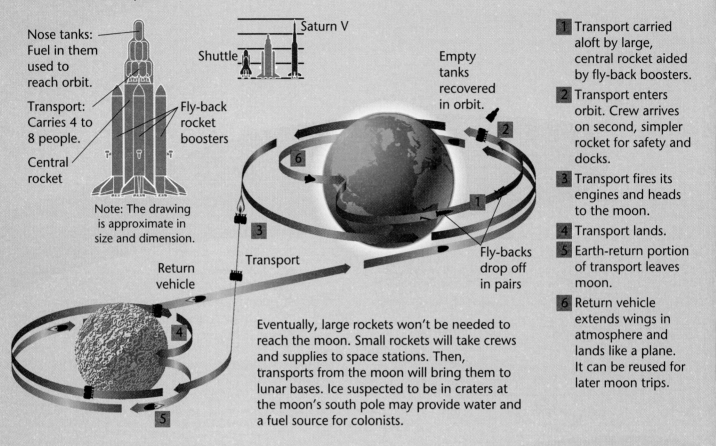

Nose tanks: Fuel in them used to reach orbit.

Saturn V

Shuttle

Transport: Carries 4 to 8 people.

Fly-back rocket boosters

Central rocket

Note: The drawing is approximate in size and dimension.

Empty tanks recovered in orbit.

Return vehicle

Transport

Fly-backs drop off in pairs

Eventually, large rockets won't be needed to reach the moon. Small rockets will take crews and supplies to space stations. Then, transports from the moon will bring them to lunar bases. Ice suspected to be in craters at the moon's south pole may provide water and a fuel source for colonists.

1 Transport carried aloft by large, central rocket aided by fly-back boosters.

2 Transport enters orbit. Crew arrives on second, simpler rocket for safety and docks.

3 Transport fires its engines and heads to the moon.

4 Transport lands.

5 Earth-return portion of transport leaves moon.

6 Return vehicle extends wings in atmosphere and lands like a plane. It can be reused for later moon trips.

2015 to 2020

Mars and beyond

Aldrin proposes a special spacecraft called a "cycler" that could reach Mars without engines or fuel. The craft would be put in orbit around the sun so that it passes by Earth and Mars on a regular basis. But first, a Mars base would be built using a reusable spacecraft with engines.

FIRST PHASE

1 Crew depart in spaceship large enough to comfortably hold them and supplies during the long journey to Mars.

2 Using its engines, the ship stops at Mars and enters orbit. Smaller craft are used to reach the planet or its moons.

3 When refueled, ship breaks orbit and heads back to Earth with returning crew. As it flies by Earth, new crew and supplies arrive and old crew leaves on smaller craft.

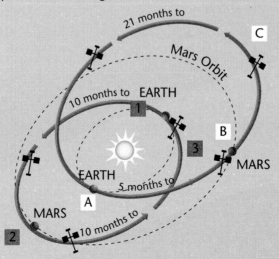

21 months to

Mars Orbit

10 months to EARTH

5 months to

EARTH

MARS

10 months to

MARS

SECOND PHASE

A Crews dock with cycler when its orbit nears Earth.

B Smaller ships depart cycler when it nears Mars. Cycler has no braking engines, so it doesn't stop.

C Cycler uses gravity of Mars to swing around the planet and back to Earth. New crews board it there.

Neil A. Armstrong

Neil Alden Armstrong was born in Wapakoneta, Ohio, on August 5, 1930. On his sixteenth birthday, Neil received his pilot's licence, which meant a great deal to him.

Neil later joined Purdue University, and in 1955 he got his aeronautical engineering degree and became a test pilot. In 1962, with great honor, he was selected as an astronaut.

Neil was later assigned as commander of Apollo 11, the first American attempt to land on the moon. Finally the day arrived. It was July 20, 1969. Armstrong and lunar module pilot Edwin E. Aldrin took off on their journey into space.

At exactly 10:56:20 p.m. Eastern time, Neil A. Armstrong planted his left foot in the rocky soil of the Sea of Tranquillity on the moon. As he did so, he said, "That's one small step for a man, one giant leap for mankind."

Brittney Andress
Grade 6

For me, writing is fun. You get to open up your imagination and see different creatures, places, and times. By writing, you have a chance to learn about things that you never knew about before.

Brittney Andress

First Human on Pluto

I start to sweat heavily.
It feels like I'm going to explode.
I touch down with a slight bump.
Dust flies everywhere.
I step out of my silver ship.
My silver suit gleams then turns brown.
For I am the first human on Pluto.

Jamie Cormier
Grade 6

Spaceship

When the spaceship goes up in the air,
It always makes me want to stare.
As it goes up in the sky
It makes me wonder why—
How it can fly.

Valerie Ridgway
Age 10

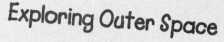

Exploring Outer Space

Once upon a time there was a scientist named Jhan Moore. He was a strong scientist who explored outer space. So one day he went to the space shuttle headquarters and talked to the manager about outer space. The manager saw that he was interested in outer space, so he asked him if he wanted to go to outer space. Then Jhan said, "I'd love to go to outer space."

The next day he came back to the headquarters to learn how to fly the space shuttle. After one week he was set, but he had to wait until Monday so he could be launched. For the next couple of days he worked out and ate lots and lots of food. Then it was Monday and he went in the space shuttle with three other people named Buzz Aldrin, Michael Collins, and Neil Armstrong. Two of the three astronauts were going to be the first people on the moon. The mission controller counted down—"5, 4, 3, 2, 1, Blast off!" Then Jhan began his trip to outer space.

Mushdaag Hashtee
Age 10

The Dream Job

"Okay, class! For today's homework assignment I want you to write about what your dream job would be," said Peter's Grade 3 teacher, Mrs. Wilamire. But Peter had no idea what to write about.

Later that day Peter stared out of his bedroom window at the dark night sky through his telescope and then he imagined himself as an astronaut, exploring the stars and making new discoveries in the universe. "That's what I want to do," said Peter quietly to himself. "I want to explore all of the different galaxies and visit new planets," continued Peter. And up to this day, Peter is following his dream, exploring the stars.

Andrew Winkler
Grade 6

Is There Life on Other Planets?

by Marion Lane
Photographed by
Gilbert Duclos

CHARACTERS
Chief Scientist
Five Scientists

SETTING: A conference room.
AT RISE: Chief Scientist and
other Scientists are seated
at conference table, their
backs to audience.

CHIEF SCIENTIST *(Rising, with back to audience)*: Ladies and gentlemen. Please come to order. I have called you here today to make an important announcement. I am sorry to tell you that after exhaustive studies, we have come to the conclusion that there cannot possibly be any life on the planet nearest us.

1ST SCIENTIST: But what about the changes in color from white to green that have been observed on the planet's surface? Don't these indicate weather changes and some kind of atmosphere?

CHIEF SCIENTIST: All tests show that there is some atmosphere on the planet, but it is not enough to sustain life as we know it.

2ND SCIENTIST: Then how do you account for the ditches or canals that have been seen with our telescopes?

CHIEF SCIENTIST: Latest viewings indicate that these are merely natural ground formations, and there is no proof whatever that they are made by any living beings.

3RD SCIENTIST: Then we must conclude that the flying saucer stories are all hoaxes?

CHIEF SCIENTIST: No, of course not. Most of these sightings have perfectly logical, scientific explanations, and the rest are the direct result of mass hysteria.

4TH SCIENTIST: Then all the strange sounds picked up on radio receivers come from our own transmitters or are produced by atmospheric pressures?

CHIEF SCIENTIST: I'm afraid so.

5TH SCIENTIST: I, for one, am extremely disappointed. I've always been sure we had neighbors on other planets, or at least on the one nearest to us. Perhaps not life as we know it, but some kind of intelligent life, totally unknown to us.

CHIEF SCIENTIST: Ladies and gentlemen, I am going to adjourn this meeting. I can see no point in discussing this matter further. The tests have been so conclusive that any intelligent person must accept the fact that there is no life on —

ALL (*Turning to audience to reveal weird masks or make-up*): Earth! (*Curtain*)

THE NIGHT OF THE POMEGRANATE

by Tim Wynne-Jones
Illustrated by June Lawrason

Harriet's solar system was a mess. She had made it—the sun and its nine planets—out of rolled-up balls of the morning newspaper. It was mounted on a sheet of green Bristol board. The Bristol board had a project about Austria on the other side. Harriet wished the background were black. Green was all wrong.

Everything about her project was wrong. The crumpled paper was coming undone. Because she had used the last of the Scotch tape on Saturn's rings, the three remaining planets had nothing to keep them scrunched up. Tiny Pluto was already bigger than Jupiter and growing by the minute. She had also run out of glue, so part of her solar system was stuck together with grape chewing gum.

Harriet's big brother, Tom, was annoyed at her because Mom made him drive her to school early with her stupid project. Dad was annoyed at her for using part of the business section. Mostly she had stuck to the want ads, but then an advertisement printed in red ink in the business section caught her eye, and she just had to have it for Mars. Harriet had a crush on Mars; that's what Tom said. She didn't even mind him saying it.

Mars was near the Earth this month. The nights had been November cold but clear as glass, and Harriet had been out to see Mars every night, which was why she hadn't got her solar system finished, why she was so tired, why Mom made Tom drive her to school. It was all Mars's fault.

She was using the tape on Ms. Krensky's desk when Clayton Beemer arrived with his dad. His solar system came from the hobby store. The planets were Styrofoam balls, all different sizes and painted the right colors. Saturn's rings were clear plastic painted over as delicately as insect wings.

Harriet looked at her own Saturn. Her rings were drooping despite all the tape. They looked like a limp skirt on a . . . on a ball of scrunched-up newspaper.

Harriet sighed. The wires that supported Clayton's planets in their black box were almost invisible. The planets seemed to float.

"What d'ya think?" Clayton asked. He beamed. Mr. Beemer beamed. Harriet guessed that *he* had made the black box with its glittery smear of stars.

She had rolled up her own project protectively when Clayton entered the classroom. Suddenly one of the planets came unstuck and fell on the floor. Clayton and Mr. Beemer looked at it.

"What's that?" asked Clayton.

"Pluto, I think," said Harriet, picking it up. She popped it in her mouth. It tasted of grape gum. "Yes, Pluto," she said. Clayton and Mr. Beemer walked away to find the best place to show off their project.

Darjit arrived next. "Hi, Harriet," she said. The project under her arm had the planets' names done in bold gold lettering. Harriet's heart sank. Pluto tasted stale and cold.

But last night Harriet had tasted pomegranates. Old Mrs. Pond had given her one while she busied herself putting on layer after layer of warm clothing and gathering the things they would need for their Mars watch.

Mrs. Pond lived in the country. She lived on the edge of the woods by a meadow that sloped down to a marsh through rough frost-licked grass and prickly ash and juniper. It was so much darker than town; good for star-gazing.

By eleven p.m. Mars was directly above the marsh, which was where Harriet and Mrs. Pond set themselves up for their vigil. They found it just where they had left it the night before: in the constellation Taurus between the Pleiades and the Hyades. But you didn't need a map to find Mars these nights. It shone like rust, neither trembling nor twinkling as the fragile stars did.

Mrs. Pond smiled and handed Harriet two folded-up golfers' chairs. "Ready?" she asked.

june

"Ready, class?" said Ms. Krensky. Everyone took their seats. Harriet placed the green Bristol board universe in front of her. It was an even worse mess than it had been when she arrived. Her solar system was ravaged.

It had started off with Pluto and then, as a joke to make Darjit laugh, she had eaten Neptune. Then Karen had come in, and Jodi and Nick and Scott.

"The planet taste test," Harriet had said, ripping off a bit of Mercury. "Umm, very spicy." By the time the bell rang there wasn't much of her project left.

Kevin started. He stood at the back of the classroom holding a green and blue marble.

"If this was Earth," he said, "then the sun would be this big—" He put the Earth in his pocket and then pulled a fat squishy yellow beach ball from a garbage bag. Everybody hooted and clapped. "And it would be at the crosswalk," he added. Everyone looked confused, so Ms. Krensky helped Kevin explain the relative distances between the Earth and the sun. "And Pluto would be eighty kilometres away from here," said Kevin. But then he wasn't sure about that, so Ms. Krensky worked it out at the board with him.

Meanwhile, using Kevin's example, the class was supposed to figure out where other planets in the solar system would be relative to the green and blue marble in Kevin's pocket. Harriet sighed.

Until last night, Harriet had never seen the inside of a pomegranate before. As she opened the hard rind, she marvelled at the bright red seeds in their cream-colored fleshy pouches.

"It's like a little secret universe all folded in on itself," said Mrs. Pond.

Harriet tasted it. With her tongue, she popped a little red bud against the roof of her mouth. The taste startled her, made her laugh.

"Tonight," Mrs. Pond said, "Mars is only seventy-seven million kilometres away." They drank a cocoa toast to that. Then she told Harriet about another time when Mars had been even closer on its orbit around the sun. She had been a girl then, and had heard on the radio the famous broadcast of "The War of the Worlds." An actor named Orson Welles had made a radio drama based on a story about Martians attacking the world, but he had made it in a series of news bulletins and reports, and a lot of people had believed it was true.

Harriet listened to Mrs. Pond and sipped her cocoa and stared at the Earth's closest neighbor and felt deliciously chilly and warm at the same time. Mars was wonderfully clear in the telescope, but even with the naked eye she could imagine canals and raging storms. She knew there weren't really Martians, but she allowed herself to imagine them anyway. She imagined one of them preparing for his invasion of the Earth, packing his laser gun, a thermos of cocoa, and a golfer's chair.

"What in heaven's name is this?" Ms. Krensky was standing at Harriet's chair staring down at the green Bristol board. There was only one planet left.

"Harriet says it's Mars." Darjit started giggling.

"And how big is Mars?" asked Ms. Krensky. Her eyes said Unsatisfactory.

"Compared to Kevin's marble Earth, Mars would be the size of a pomegranate seed, including the juicy red pulp," said Harriet. Ms. Krensky walked to the front of the class. She turned at her desk. Was there the hint of a smile on her face?

"And where is it?" she asked, raising an eyebrow.

Harriet looked at the calculations she had done on a corner of the green Bristol board. "If the sun was at the crosswalk," said Harriet, "then Mars would be much closer. Over there." She pointed out the window at the slide in the kindergarten playground. Some of the class actually looked out the window to see if they could see it.

"You *can* see Mars," said Harriet. "Sometimes." Now she was sure she saw Ms. Krensky smile.

"How many of you have seen Mars?" the teacher asked. Only Harriet and Randy Pilcher put up their hands. But Randy had only seen it on the movie *Total Recall*.

"Last night was a special night, I believe," said Ms. Krensky, crossing her arms and leaning against her desk. Harriet nodded. "Tell us about it, Harriet," said the teacher.

So Harriet did. She told them all about Mrs. Pond and the Mars watch. She started with the pomegranate.

ABOUT THE AUTHOR   TIM WYNNE-JONES

Tim Wynne-Jones and his family immigrated to Canada from England in 1952. They settled first in British Columbia and later in Ontario. Since the 1970s, Tim has earned recognition not only as a writer but also as a book designer, illustrator, and performing artist. His book *Some of the Kinder Planets* won both the Governor General's Award and the Canadian Library Association Children's Book of the Year Award in 1993.

IT CAME FROM OUTER SPACE

by Terence Dickinson

A few minutes before sunset on June 14, 1994, Stéphane Forcier of St-Robert, PQ, was riding home on his bicycle. Suddenly he heard something whoosh down from the sky and thump onto the ground. In a field nearby, he saw a group of cows standing in a circle looking at something. When he went to investigate, he found a hole—like a freshly dug hole for a fence post. At the bottom of the hole was a rock the size of a grapefruit. It was a meteorite — a rock from outer space that had just hit Earth! There are billions of other rocks deep in space, just like the one Stéphane found. But don't you worry about being conked in the head by a meteorite. In recorded history only two people have ever been hit by one and they have both lived to tell the tale!

What Is a Meteorite?

Have you ever seen a shooting star flash across the night sky? Shooting stars aren't really stars. In fact, they have nothing to do with stars at all. They're bits of rocky material left over from when the planets formed billions of years ago. When one of these pieces hits Earth's atmosphere, it usually burns up in a second or two. That quick flash of light is called a "meteor." Most meteors are tiny objects, the size of a peanut or smaller. Sometimes a bigger chunk plunges into the atmosphere and does not completely burn up. If it reaches the Earth's surface, it's called a "meteorite." Meteorites are sometimes made of rock, a lot like Earth rocks, or of metals such as iron and nickel that look very different from any rock you'd find on Earth.

Every year around August 11, there is a meteor "shower" called the Perseids. Up to fifty meteors per hour can be seen if the sky is clear and dark. The particles that cause meteor showers are quite small and no Perseid meteor has ever reached the ground. Another meteor shower, called the Geminids, is seen in mid-December.

In December 1994, astronomers used a telescope at Kitt Peak Observatory in Arizona to track a space boulder the size of a house! It whizzed right between Earth and the moon. That was the first time an object of that size has ever been seen so close to Earth.

In 1908, a giant space boulder broke into Earth's atmosphere over central Siberia. When the boulder was about 10 km above Earth's surface, it exploded. The explosion was so powerful that a man standing 60 km away was thrown to the ground. And millions of trees were flattened like broken matchsticks.

A giant crater 175 km wide has been discovered in Mexico's Yucatan Peninsula. An asteroid or comet that hit Earth 65 million years ago may have blasted out this crater. Some scientists think it's the "killer crater" that wiped out the dinosaurs.

Meteorites come from the asteroid belt located between the orbits of Mars and Jupiter. They're chunks of asteroid rock that are knocked off when millions of asteroids in the belt bang into each other.

About five hundred meteorites hit Earth's surface every year. Most drop in oceans. Others fall on deserts, forests, and other areas with few humans. Only a few of those that hit land are ever found. And the ones that are found are usually only the size of a golf ball or a baseball.

On a dark night in the country, far from city lights, you can see about five meteors, or shooting stars, every hour if you watch carefully. Occasionally, you might see a really bright one. Astronomers call these "fireballs." A bright fireball may look like it is coming down close to you, but it's usually many kilometres up in the sky.

Meteor Speak

meteor: the correct name for a shooting star

meteoroid: any small body in space that creates meteors when plunging through the atmosphere

meteorite: a chunk of rock from space that reaches Earth's surface

Meteoritics: the study of all of the above

Meteorology: the science of weather forecasting (it's got nothing to do with meteors!)

fireball: a brilliant meteor

asteroid: any rocky object smaller than a planet and larger than a meteoroid that orbits the sun inside the orbit of Jupiter (the majority of asteroids are between the orbits of Mars and Jupiter)

comet: any object containing large amounts of ice that orbits the sun (comets that approach the sun closer than Jupiter does can develop vapor tails)

Scientists estimate that 200 000 tonnes of meteoric material collide with Earth each year. Most of it is immediately burned up as meteors. Some very tiny particles may actually reach the ground. The dust under your bed could have real meteorite material from space mixed in with it!

Canada has more meteorite craters than any other country in the world. This is because most of Canada is made of very old rock that still shows the scars of ancient impacts. There are twenty-six known craters in Canada. The biggest is 200 km wide. It's in Sudbury, ON, and it's almost two billion years old!

Our Solar System: News and Views

The solar system is Earth's address in the Milky Way galaxy. It's definitely not a quiet neighborhood! Read on for news and views about the action in our own backyard.

The Sun: Patterns of heavenly chaos

By Dan Falk
The Globe and Mail
April 29,1995

Life on Earth is a delicate affair. The planet's average temperature is about 15 degrees. If it were to fall just a few degrees, many plants and animals would die. If it were to rise the same amount, changes in ocean currents could have a devastating effect on marine life and the entire food chain. Even a one-degree increase could start to melt the polar ice caps, with disastrous results for low-lying areas.

With the growing concern over the influence of human activity on climate change, it's easy to overlook another factor—perhaps a more important one—that has a direct influence on the Earth's ability to sustain life: the sun.

From our perspective, some 150 million kilometres away, the sun may appear constant and stable. But viewed up close, it is a chaotic and violent place. Fierce magnetic storms hurl streams of electrically charged particles thousands of kilometres above its surface, while currents in the interior churn the dense layers of gas below. And deep within the core, a nuclear furnace produces the energy that drives the solar engine.

Fortunately for scientists trying to make sense of solar activity, there are definite patterns that emerge from the chaos. Astronomers have found that many of the sun's physical properties occur in cycles. The most apparent cycle is linked to magnetic activity on the sun's surface and to the appearance of dark regions known as sunspots. The number of sunspots reaches a maximum every eleven years.

Counting sunspots is one thing. Detecting more subtle changes in the sun's temperature and magnetic fields is more difficult. To study any periodic change, astronomers have to observe many cycles. That means decades of observations.

McGill scientist tries to unlock mystery of life on Mars

Canadian Press
August 9, 1996

The next step in solving the great puzzle of whether humans have found signs of long-dead and unintelligent life on Mars will partly be taken under electron microscopes at McGill University.

Those steps will be handled by Dr. Hojatollah Vali, a 49-year-old Iranian-born, German-trained bio-geologist, whose skills at creating images of rock surfaces have gained him considerable attention from NASA.

Vali is a pioneer at making thin casts of rock surfaces using a combination of platinum and carbon.

These casts, as thin as 1/500th of the thickness of a hair, produced the remarkable images shown at the news conference in Washington where NASA presented evidence that life, or at least bacteria, may have existed on Mars.

The scientists used a variety of chemical tests to justify their claims they had seen the fossilized remains of microbes in a meteorite discovered in Antarctica.

It was Vali's technique of carbon-platinum masking to analyze rocks at McGill that took him to the Johnson Space Center in Houston for the secret scientific project.

Comet collision blinds scopes
Brilliant flash as three-kilometre chunk hits Jupiter

By Wallace Immen
The Globe and Mail
July 19, 1994

TORONTO — A giant chunk of a comet exploding in the atmosphere of Jupiter caused such a brilliant flash it blinded instruments on Earth, scientists reported yesterday.

Fragment G—at three kilometres in diameter the largest of twenty-one pieces of the comet Shoemaker-Levy 9 expected to crash into the planet this week—caused an explosion yesterday morning estimated at six million megatons of TNT. That's six hundred times more power than could be released by all the nuclear bombs stockpiled on Earth, said astronomer Eugene Shoemaker, one of the co-discoverers of the comet.

Four of the eight fragments to hit so far have set up a line of persistent storms that could cause long-lasting changes in the atmosphere, Mr. Shoemaker speculated.

He said their fiery plumes have left dark splotches, each at least the

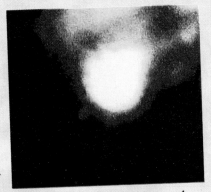

COLLISION/*Infrared image shows the flare that developed after the collision between fragment G of comet Shoemaker-Levy 9 and Jupiter. (NASA)*

size of Earth, in the giant planet's gaseous atmosphere.

Astronomers say they still don't know what the spots are made of or how long they might last.

To Mars, courtesy of our sponsor

Editorial
The Globe and Mail
July 19, 1994

This is a week in which the past and the present of space exploration have almost literally crashed into one another.

The Hubble Space Telescope has functioned as our eye on Jupiter. It has flashed back image after image of mountain-sized pieces of comet Shoemaker-Levy 9 smashing into Jupiter.

At the same time, and often in the same time slot, humanity has begun to commemorate the twenty-fifth anniversary of the first landing on the moon. The reprise of the grainy, black-and-white pictures of Neil Armstrong stepping down onto the dusty lunar face recaptures the simple awe of the thing.

After millennia of wondering what the night's shining beacon really was, Mr. Armstrong and fellow spacefarer Buzz Aldrin finally took us to a place where no woman, or man, or curious cat had ever gone before. For those enthralled with space, both of this week's events seem to carry the same message.

Our need to know consumes us. Exploring the universe is our destiny, because exploration is the essence of the human soul. And yet when we look back at men awkwardly walking on the moon and look forward at comets crashing into Jupiter, it is also clear that curiosity—particularly curiosity about space—doesn't entirely define humanity.

We want people on the moon and an end to starvation on Earth. We want to see comets ripple through the Jovian atmosphere and a stop to the massacres in Rwanda. We want, we want, we want—but what can we afford?

That is the true question. How do people living in a world in which pain and poverty and disease shout with such fearful voices ever decide how much of their limited treasuries should be given over to raw curiosity? If a trip to Mars costs $500-billion, is there any way of deciding how to balance this enormous expense against the more mundane good those billions could buy?

MARTIAN SUNSET/*This color image of the Martian surface was taken by Viking Lander 1 about 15 minutes before sunset. (NASA)*

There is clearly no simple answer, but there may be a way to redefine the question in such a way that the various human goods do not so clearly clash with one another. Democratic governments by their very nature must make decisions based on some goulash of competing public interests. Private organizations, on the other hand, are not so clearly limited.

Perhaps future curiosity-driven space exploration should be more of a mixed economy. Governments would clearly have to pay much of the cost, but could not some consideration be given to enticing private industry to participate? If a baseball card is worth nearly half a million dollars, how much would collectors pay for a kilogram of Martian soil?

And what about the space-exploration equivalent of selling the movie rights? The television revenues for the next summer Olympics are expected to bring in $1-billion. In a difficult economic climate, wouldn't it also make sense to put out to tender the rights to broadcast the voyages of human discovery? And while it will sound terribly crass to purists, if ads for Coca-Cola and BMW and Hitachi have to be emblazoned across a rocket's mid-section to get the humans to Mars or the moons of Jupiter, so be it.

Curiosity, dirty emotion that it is, won't even know it is supposed to be embarrassed.

Don't believe everything you read about comets

Terence Dickinson
The Toronto Star
September 25, 1994

Earlier this month a news story distributed by the Reuters news service said that fragments of Comet Machholz-2 "could be on a collision course with Earth."

The item was carried in many newspapers with the headline, "New comet coming our way." The story deserved the prominent coverage it received—if it was accurate. But it wasn't. The comet was not coming anywhere near the Earth, now or anytime in the future that could be predicted. Just how Reuters got this story so screwed up is a tale in itself.

Comet Machholz-2 was discovered in August during a visual comet search by California amateur astronomer Don Machholz. The object was very faint, well below naked-eye visibility, and not much different than dozens of comets seen before. It was nowhere near Earth. In fact, when the Reuters story hit, it was moving *away* from it.

But early this month, astronomers' attention was drawn to this otherwise unremarkable comet when it broke into five pieces and brightened by a factor of ten over less than three days.

Orbit calculations revealed that Comet Machholz-2 is in a five-year orbit of the sun, a route that passes near Jupiter. Apparently, Jupiter's immense gravity had disrupted this object in a way similar to the breakup of Comet Shoemaker-Levy, the comet that crashed into Jupiter in July.

It was at this point that astronomers started receiving calls, one of which, from a *Sunday Telegraph* reporter in England, went to Duncan Steel of the Anglo-Australian Observatory. Steel correctly pointed out that because the comet passed close to Jupiter every five years, its orbit is affected by Jupiter's gravity. Conceivably, it could be diverted into a trajectory toward Earth. Not now. Sometime. Maybe. Perhaps. Conceivably.

But the first sentence in the story carried by Reuters read: "Fragments from a newly discovered comet are under intense observations by astronomers who believe they could be on a collision course with Earth."

That's deliberate sensationalism. Who cares? Well, *I* care that people will be wondering when the comet will hit Earth, and why they aren't hearing more about it.

Newspapers trust the accuracy of what they receive through major news services. Occasionally, though, a boner gets through.

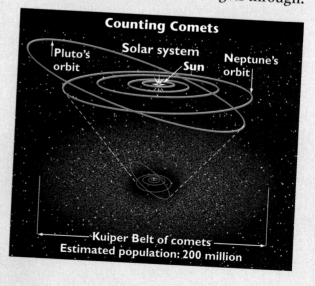

Counting Comets

Pluto's orbit • Solar system • Sun • Neptune's orbit

←— Kuiper Belt of comets —→
Estimated population: 200 million

A giant leap fades into history

By Stephen Strauss
Science Reporter
The Globe and Mail
July 20, 1994

Today marks one of the most surprising reversals of the 20th century.

Twenty-five years after the first human foot embedded itself in the dead, dusty surface of the moon, the event seems to be shrinking in human consciousness. For people who were born after the event, or were too young to remember it clearly, Neil Armstrong's giant leap for mankind has little or no emotional resonance.

"Did it make a difference to life on Earth? I don't think so. As long as I can't go to the moon, what difference does it make in my personal life?" is the shoulder-shrugging response of Farinaz Razi, a 24-year-old Toronto ballet dancer.

"It's become a standard measure of what we haven't accomplished in other areas. You know, 'Man can land on the moon but not find a cure for...'" said Sioban McAneney, 28, who works for Loblaws in Ottawa. Her only vague memory of the event was how her parents' rapt interest in the moon-walking and subsequent days of coverage cut into the television shows she really wanted to watch.

High-school students can't remember hearing any discussion of the events in their classes. Nobody is sure when the last trip was made and how many have gone.

While interviews with a dozen people who have no moon-walking imprint in their memories is hardly scientific polling, the deflation of man's first trip to another world is also a theme which constantly crops up in discussions with space historians and analysts.

For the media-conscious, television—which allowed the landing to be the most watched event of its time—has progressively undermined its significance. *Star Trek* and all its sci-fi cousins have created the illusion that we have already traipsed about more and better worlds than one barren satellite.

LUNAR LANDING/*Twenty-five years ago the moon shot captured the imagination of millions. These days, it all seems a bit tawdry.*

"The imagination has created experiences which have surpassed the real one. It is hard for people to differentiate what was real from what is not," acknowledged John Logsdon, space policy analyst at George Washington University in Washington.

It is an assessment that Michael Tokunaga, 16, of Edmonton agrees with. "They go to spectacular places on TV, but the moon is just kind of dry and dusty and kind of boring," he reflected.

Letters to the Editor
The Globe and Mail
July 27, 1994

Man on the moon

I was offended by Stephen Strauss's article A Giant Leap Fades Into History (July 20).

Perhaps Mr. Strauss's memory is not long enough or clear enough to recall accurately the events of the 1960s leading up to the moon landing 25 years ago. It marked both the technological pinnacle of mankind's development and a turning point in the domestic policies of Western society toward commonplace, mundane and, I would suggest, irreconcilable problems that have been with us for centuries.

The Apollo missions marked an almost 40-year period of intense technological effort by teams of people in pursuit of a common goal. With the exception of the Second World War, no other endeavor has ever demonstrated the kind of sustained, persistent commitment to excellence demonstrated by all of the people connected with the Apollo program.

To belittle their accomplishment does an injustice to the memory of those who died during the development of the Apollo missions and illustrates why our society will likely never achieve the greatness it once had. The special effects of *Star Wars* and *Star Trek* films will remain nothing more than fantasy unless others can be encouraged to fund and support the next "great leap."

R.K. McCartney, Toronto

CBC News
March 7, 1996

Hubble Space Telescope Pictures of Pluto

Pluto
Hubble Space Telescope · Faint Object Camera

PROGRAM: THE NATIONAL

NETWORK: CBC

TIME: 22:00:00 ET to 22:23:00 ET

HOST: ALISON SMITH

GUEST: Bob McDonald, Host, "Quirks and Quarks"

ALISON SMITH: Some astonishing news, tonight, from the world of science. New pictures, from the Hubble Space Telescope, are raising questions about Pluto. Some experts believe that the ninth planet may not be a planet at all.

To explain this story, we're joined by Bob McDonald, the host of the CBC's Radio Science Program "Quirks and Quarks." Bob, what did Hubble see?

BOB McDONALD: Well, Alison, Hubble has transformed Pluto, which has been nothing more than a tiny dot in our telescopes for the last sixty-six years since it was discovered, into a world of which we're just beginning to see surface details. And, if we go to the pictures, you'll see what I mean.

The first image is a surface map of Pluto. And, you can see that it just has light and dark markings on its surface. Pluto is a tiny ice world. It's smaller than our moon, and it's believed that these light and dark markings are just different kinds of ice. The white stuff is clean, and the dark stuff might be dirty.

Now they took this map, and they wrapped it into a sphere, so that we can see Pluto rotating, and we've got a polarized cap at the top, and then these light and dark markings. What they need to do, now, is figure out what those light and dark markings are.

SMITH: So, why do some people think Pluto is not a planet?

McDONALD: Well, it's possible that Pluto is actually a captured object that came from outside the solar system. Because it's made of ice, it's not like other planets, and we know that, beyond our solar system, we're surrounded by a bunch of ice balls. Now, some of them occasionally wander in towards the sun, and they develop tails and they become comets that we see in our night sky. So, it's possible that Pluto wandered in, but it passed close to Neptune, and Neptune then threw it into the orbit that it's in today.

So, although it does go around the sun like a planet, and it has a moon like a planet, it may just be a very different kind, with a different beginning.

SMITH: Thanks very much, Bob.

McDONALD: OK, Alison.

Saturn: Lord of the Rings

by Jerry Emory

Saturn has fascinated scientists and stargazers for centuries, but it took spacecraft and modern telescopes to help astronomers unlock some of the planet's secrets. Photographs taken by Pioneer and Voyager spacecraft show that Saturn has seven large rings, not two as scientists once believed.

Saturn's seven icy rings are made of thousands of smaller ringlets. The rings are only around ninety metres thick, and they extend about 420 000 kilometres into space. The most substantial outer ring, called the F ring, twists and curls around Saturn. Keep reading to learn more about the second-largest planet in the solar system.

On a clear moonless night, go out to a dark place away from city lights. Gaze across millions of kilometres of space and try to spot Saturn. Use a current star chart from your local newspaper to help you. You're looking for a bright, yellowish object that doesn't twinkle or flicker—Saturn.

The solar system has nine planets. Saturn, the most distant planet visible to the naked eye, is the sixth planet from the sun. Saturn is the largest planet after Jupiter. About 840 Earths could fit inside it. Yet Saturn is relatively lightweight. It would float on water, if you could find an ocean big enough to hold it. Saturn is made mostly of gases—hydrogen and helium. Lower in its atmosphere are liquids. The planet core may be solid.

Saturn is surrounded by a dull, yellow haze. But beneath its pale veil, the planet is hopping! Winds race around Saturn's equator faster than 450 metres per second. That's about ten times stronger than a hurricane on Earth. And Saturn is cold! Temperatures there can drop to an estimated -184°C.

Big, cold, and full of gas, Saturn is slower than Earth in one way but faster in another. Saturn takes about thirty Earth years to orbit the sun. Earth takes only one year. But Saturn rotates on its axis every ten hours and thirty minutes. Earth takes twenty-four hours to rotate.

And those rings! Other planets—Jupiter, Uranus, Neptune—have cosmic hula hoops, but theirs are small compared to Saturn's. Scientists aren't sure why Saturn's rings are so big. They do know the rings contain trillions of ice particles. The particles range from dust-size to the size of large buildings.

The final count isn't in yet, but scientists believe Saturn has at least twenty moons—more than any other planet. Titan, the largest, is the only moon in the solar system that has an atmosphere. Titan's air contains no oxygen. And at around -180°C, the temperature on Titan is much too cold to support life. But Titan does have methane and other organic materials found in living things. Scientists believe that Titan's conditions may have been similar to Earth's during Earth's formation. If so, what we learn about Saturn and its moons may reveal information about our own planet.

Saturn and some of its moons.

New View of Hot Stuff

Using cameras mounted on telescopes and special photographic techniques, astronomers have detected heat sources on Saturn (shown in red). The planet is hotter than its rings. And the rings nearest the planet (yellow) are hotter than the outer rings (blue).

Rings Around the Planet

About once every fifteen years, Saturn tilts edge-on toward Earth. In the photograph at right, Saturn's rings appear as a dark band across the planet's middle.

Space Man

Italian-born astronomer Giovanni Cassini discovered a gap between two of Saturn's rings in 1675. Scientists call that gap the Cassini Division. Cassini also discovered four of the planet's moons.

News Flash: Saturn Sports a Great White Spot

Saturn watchers in 1990 saw a spectacular white spot take form. Scientists believe storms cause such spots when warm gases rise above the planet. The rising gases cool, forming a mass of swirling ammonia crystals. The crystals are visible from Earth because they reflect light better than the rest of Saturn's gases. This kind of storm occurs about once every thirty years.

Pushing and Pulling the Thin White Line

Saturn's F ring looks like a long string let loose by an astronaut (see photograph at right). This ring on the outer edge of the planet's ring system twists, wiggles, and wobbles. Scientists believe two "shepherd moons" sandwich the F ring and keep it in line. The force of gravity between the two moons may give the ring stability.

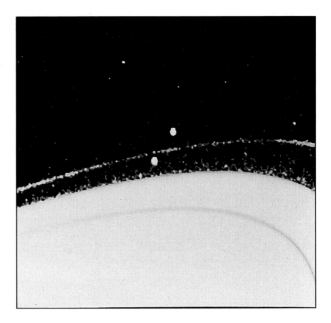

Bright Site: Moon Rivers

Images taken with the Hubble Space Telescope provide information about Titan, Saturn's largest moon. In one such image (left), the dark areas may be liquid methane rivers or seas. The bright area may be an area of frozen methane and nitrogen the size of Australia.

New Spacecraft and a Planetary Probe

The spacecraft Cassini took off in October 1997. It will fly by Venus and Jupiter. Then it will reach Saturn in July 2004. The Cassini will drop a probe named Huygens to Titan's surface, where it will study the moon and its atmosphere. The probe is named for Christian Huygens, the Dutch astronomer who discovered Titan in 1659.

Brandon Gibson

> I think writing is a great challenge and work for the mind.

Jupiter

As I descend to Jupiter below,
I thrust into the gas, Jupiter's gas.
The ice is magnificent, and glowing.
I send a probe to test the ground.
Slowly I turn to the viewer,
It creeps to the planet below.
The pressure is great but the probe is greater.
CRUNCH!
The probe is gone, crushed like a paper cup.

Brandon Gibson
Grade 6

Mercury

My atmosphere almost burned away
Extremely thin the people say
Red hot heat from the sun
Cups of air flying high
Up high into the night sky
Running volcanoes
Years burning as quick as a wink.

Stacey Gagnon
Grade 6

The Solar System

Stars are giant balls of hot, glowing gas. There are many millions of stars in space. We can see about two thousand of them on a clear night. A telescope reveals millions more.

All the stars except one can be seen only at night. The one that shows up in the daytime is the sun. In fact, the sun is just average in brightness, hotness, and size. Why, then, does it look so bright? Why does it look so much bigger than other stars? The answer is that the sun is much closer to us than the other stars.

Stars are grouped together in formations called galaxies. The sun belongs to the Milky Way galaxy.

Planets are objects that orbit a star. Other stars besides the sun may have planets. The sun has nine known planets.

Mercury is the planet closest to the sun. Venus comes second. Our home planet—Earth—comes third. Then comes Mars, Jupiter, Saturn, Uranus, Neptune, and Pluto.

Seven of the nine planets have moons that orbit them. Only Venus and Mercury have no moons.

The planets do not shine by their own light, like the stars. They reflect the light of the sun.

The sun and all objects that orbit it are called the solar system. The sun is the biggest object in the solar system. The planets and their moons are the solar system's other main objects.

Now you know more about the solar system.

Sana Rehman
Grade 6

Student Writing

How Fisher Went to the Skyland
The Origin of the Big Dipper

by Joseph Bruchac
Illustrated by Kasia Charko

Fisher was a great hunter. He was not big, but he was known for his determination and was regarded as one with great power. Fisher's son wanted to be a great hunter also. One day the son went out to try to catch something. It was not easy, for the snow was very deep and it was very cold everywhere. In those days it was always winter on the Earth and there was no such thing as warm weather. The son hunted a long time with no luck. Finally, though, he saw a squirrel. As quietly as he could he sneaked up and then pounced, catching the squirrel between his paws. Before he could kill it, though, the squirrel spoke to him.

"Grandson," said the squirrel, "don't kill me. I can give you some good advice."

"Speak then," said the young fisher.

"I see that you are shivering from the cold. If you do what I tell you, we may

52

all enjoy warm weather. Then it will be easy for all of us to find food and not starve as we are doing now."

"Tell me what to do, Grandfather," the young fisher said, letting the squirrel go.

The squirrel climbed quickly up onto a high branch and then spoke again. "Go home and say nothing. Just sit down in your lodge and begin to weep. Your mother will ask you what is wrong, but you must not answer her. If she tries to comfort you or give you food, you must refuse it. When your father comes home, he will ask you why you are weeping. Then you can speak. Tell him the winds are too cold and the snow is too deep. Tell him that he must bring warm weather to the Earth."

So the young fisher went home. He sat in the corner of the lodge and cried. His mother asked what was wrong, but he did not answer. She offered him food, but he pushed it away. When his father returned and saw his only son weeping, he went to his side.

"What is wrong, son?" Fisher said. Then the young fisher said what the squirrel had told him to say.

"I am weeping because the wind is too cold and the snow is too deep. We are all starving because of the winter. I want you to use your powers to bring the warm weather."

"The thing you are asking of me is hard to do," said Fisher, "but you are right. I will do all I can to grant your wish."

Then Fisher had a great feast. He invited all of his friends and told them what he planned to do.

"I am going to go to the place where the skyland is closest to the Earth," he said. "There in the skyland the people have all the warm weather. I intend to go there to bring some of that warm weather back. Then the snow will go away and we will have plenty to eat."

All of Fisher's friends were pleased and offered to go with him. So when Fisher set out, he took the strongest of his friends along. Those friends were Otter, Lynx, and Wolverine.

The four of them travelled for a long time through the snow. They went toward the mountains, higher and higher each day. Fisher had with him a pack filled with dried venison and they slept at night buried under the snow. At last, after many, many days, they came to the highest mountain and climbed to its top. Then Fisher took a pipe and tobacco out of his pouch.

"We must offer our smoke to the Four Directions," Fisher said. The four of them smoked and sent their prayers to Gitchee Manitou, asking for success. The sky was very close above them, but they had to find some way to break through into the land above. "We must jump up," said Fisher. "Who will go first?"

"I will try," said Otter. He leaped up and struck the sky but did not break through. Instead he fell back and slid on his belly all the way to the bottom of the mountain. To this day all otters slide like that in the snow.

"Now it is my turn," said Lynx. He jumped too, striking hard against the sky and falling back unconscious. Fisher tried then, but even he did not have enough power.

"Now it is your turn," said Fisher to Wolverine. "You are the strongest of us all."

Wolverine leaped. He struck hard against the sky and fell back, but he did not give up. He leaped again and again until he had made a crack in the sky. Once more he leaped and finally broke through. Fisher jumped through the hole in the sky after him.

The skyland was a beautiful place. It was warm and sunny, and there were plants and flowers of all kinds growing. They could hear the singing of birds all around them, but they could see no people. They went farther and found many long lodges. When they looked inside, they found that there were cages in the lodges. Each cage held a different bird.

"These will make for fine hunting," Fisher said. "Let us set them free."

Quickly Wolverine and Fisher chewed through the rawhide that bound the cages together and freed the birds. The birds all flew down through the hole in the sky. So there are many kinds of birds in the world today.

Wolverine and Fisher now began to make the hole in the skyland bigger. The warmth of the skyland began to fall through the hole and the land below began to grow warmer. The snow began to melt and the grass and plants beneath the snow began to turn green.

But the sky people came out when they saw what was happening. They ran toward Wolverine and Fisher, shouting loudly.

"Thieves," they shouted. "Stop taking our warm weather!"

Wolverine jumped back through the hole to escape, but Fisher kept making the hole bigger. He knew that if he didn't make it big enough, the sky people would quickly close the hole again and it would be winter again in the land below. He chewed the hole larger and larger. Finally, just when the sky people were very close, he stopped.

The hole was big enough for enough warm weather for half of the year to escape through, but it was not big enough for enough warm weather to last all the time. That is why the winter still comes back every year. Fisher knew that the sky people might try to close the hole in the sky. He had to take their attention away from it and so he taunted them.

"I am Fisher, the great hunter," he said. "You cannot catch me." Then he ran to the tallest tree in the skyland. All the sky people ran after him. Just as they were about to grab him, he leaped up into the tree and climbed to the highest branches, where no one could follow.

At first the sky people did not know what to do. Then they began to shoot arrows at him. But Fisher wasn't hurt, for he had a special power. There was only one place on his tail where an arrow could kill him. Finally, though, the sky people guessed where his magic was and shot at that place. An arrow struck the fatal spot. Fisher turned over on his back and began to fall.

But Fisher never struck the Earth. Gitchee Manitou took pity on him because he had kept his promise and done something to help all the people. Gitchee Manitou placed Fisher high up in the sky among the stars.

If you look up into the sky, you can still see him, even though some people call that pattern of stars The Big Dipper. Every year he crosses the sky. When the arrow strikes him, he rolls over onto his back in the winter sky. But when the winter is almost ended, he faithfully turns to his feet and starts out once more on his long journey to bring the warm weather back to the Earth.

ABOUT THE AUTHOR   JOSEPH BRUCHAC

Joseph Bruchac began his writing career by writing poems for his second-grade teacher. Much later, when he left home to go to college, he began looking for Native elders who could tell him the traditional stories. He started writing them down after he had children of his own to pass them on to. His advice to anyone who wants to be a writer is: "You have to do it one page at a time, and you have to keep on doing it. You take one step to climb a mountain."

Seeing ▶ Stars

by Robert Schemenauer

Astronomers, scientists who study the stars, see with many eyes. They see in the dark better than cats can. With their ordinary eyes, they look through *optical telescopes*, instruments with lenses that collect and focus visible light. Astronomers attach cameras to these telescopes to take pictures of celestial objects like stars.

However, the secret behind some of the most spectacular photographs of starry objects is the different kinds of instruments used to record the images. For example, the "eye" of a *radio telescope* "sees" low-energy photons (tiny bundles of light energy) from stars and other objects in space. Astronomers use *radar*, which emits beams of radio waves, to "see" the surface of the moon and planets. They use other kinds of instruments to look at heat and other types of radiation emitted by stars. From all these "eyes" come the spectacular star images people love to look at.

Years of Light

Because the universe is so vast, astronomers use a special way of measuring distances. The basic unit is the light-year, the distance light travels in a year. That's 9.46 trillion kilometres! The interesting thing about light-years is that they measure both distance and time. When we see the light from very distant stars, we are actually seeing them as they were many millions of years ago.

The Sun's Corona

The sun is constantly throwing off particles. Some stay near the sun and form its corona, others are fired off into space as the *solar wind*. Large streamers such as these are often seen coming from the sun. This false-color picture was taken by an instrument on board the Solar and Heliospheric Observatory. This observatory orbits a point in space ahead of the Earth in its orbit. This keeps its view of the sun from ever being blocked by the Earth.

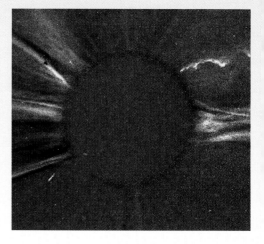

The Hubble Space Telescope

Optical telescopes that sit on the Earth's surface have to look through the atmosphere. Clouds, dust, and layers of air with different temperatures all cause problems. They limit the sharpness of the images that optical telescopes receive. The Hubble Space Telescope is in orbit above the Earth's atmosphere and can take exceptional pictures. It was put in space by the crew of the space shuttle *Discovery* on April 25, 1990. The telescope has three optical cameras, and two *spectrographs*, instruments that determine the chemical composition and other properties of astronomical objects.

The Milky Way's Centre

Our sun is one of one hundred billion stars in the Milky Way galaxy. The soft band of light in the night sky that is called the Milky Way is actually the edge-on view of our galaxy. This dramatic picture of the centre of the Milky Way galaxy was taken by the Cosmic Background Explorer (COBE) satellite. This is an *infrared* image, which means that the light used to make it has much longer wavelengths than ordinary visible light. Infrared rays carry heat radiation, so that is what is being recorded in this image. It was taken by the Diffuse InfraRed Background Experiment on COBE.

The 'Ghost of Jupiter' Planetary Nebula

Astronomers often use names from Earth or the solar system to name distant objects in space. This *nebula* is 1400 light-years away from the planet Jupiter for which it is named. A nebula is a cloud of gas and dust in a galaxy and can have many fantastic shapes and colors.

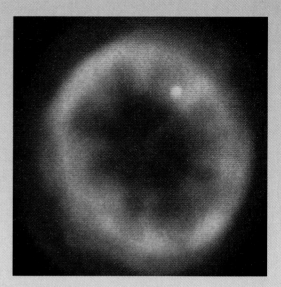

Near-Infrared Mapping Spectrometer

The Near-Infrared Mapping Spectrometer is an instrument that flies on spacecraft, such as the Galileo space probe. It is a combination of a telescope and a *spectrometer*. It was designed to examine the chemical composition of the atmosphere of the planet Jupiter. It will also measure the mineral composition of the surfaces of the moons of Jupiter.

Canada-France-Hawaii Telescope

Modern telescopes are very costly and complex. Countries often combine their efforts in order to produce the best telescope possible. They also have to choose the best observing location. This is usually on a mountaintop in a remote area. The Canada-France-Hawaii Telescope is located on top of the Mauna Kea volcano on the island of Hawaii for just this reason.

The Triple Rings of Supernova 1987A

This spectacular picture of rings of glowing gas was taken by the Hubble Space Telescope. This *supernova*, or exploded star, is 169 000 light-years away in the galaxy called the Large Magellanic Cloud. The rings were created by the explosion, but why the gas is ring-shaped is not well understood. The reason may involve a *black*

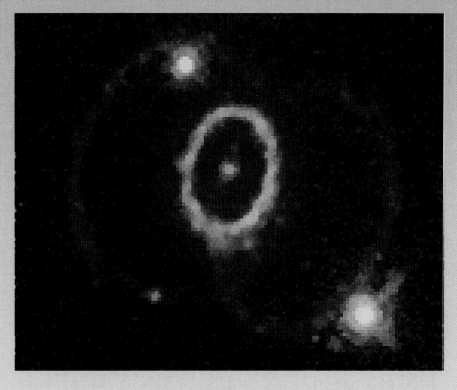

hole or a *neutron star*. A black hole is an object formed by the collapse of a star. It has such strong gravity that even light cannot escape from it. A neutron star is formed by the collapse of a supergiant star. It contains only neutrons, which are atomic particles with no electrical charge.

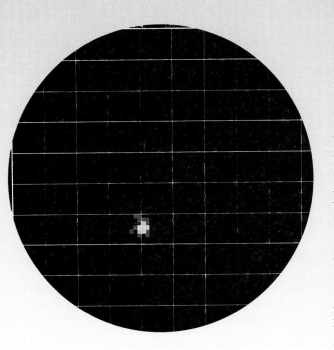

Quasar 3C279

Quasars (quasi-stellar objects) are very strange objects in the far reaches of space. Some of them are more than ten billion light-years away. A quasar may be a galaxy that has a black hole at its centre. If we look for these distant objects with optical telescopes, they appear as faint patches of light. However, NASA's orbiting Compton Gamma Ray Observatory took this impressive picture of quasar 3C279 in 1991. At that time, the quasar was emitting a large amount of gamma rays, the most energetic type of radiation. Nobody knows why this quasar emitted so much energy for a short time.

X-Ray Picture of the Pleiades Star Cluster

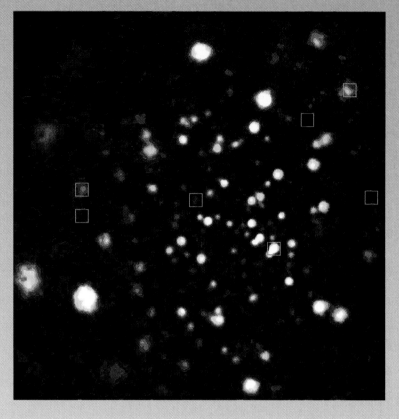

The Pleiades star cluster is a beautiful group of stars in the constellation of Taurus. It can be seen with the naked eye. To the X-ray telescopes on the orbiting Röntgen Satellite Observatory, named for the discoverer of X-rays, the Pleiades have a different look. When the X-ray energy bands are translated into colors, we see which stars emit the most X-ray energy. The energy is related to the temperature of the corona, the outer portion of the star.

The Cartwheel Galaxy

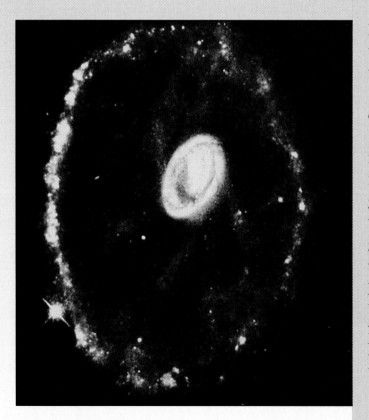

Five hundred million light-years away from Earth, in the constellation of Sculptor, two galaxies collided. The result was the Cartwheel Galaxy, which itself is 100 000 light-years in diameter. When one galaxy of stars passes through another, the gravitational fields of the stars are affected. Star positions change, and waves of new stars can be formed. This is what happened here. The picture was taken by the Hubble Space Telescope.

Deneb

Cygnus X-1

Albireo

Black Holes and
TiME TUNNELS

by David Darling
Illustrated by Dave McKay

High in the sky on a clear fall evening is the constellation of Cygnus the swan. The end of the swan's tail is marked by the bright star Deneb. Slightly ahead of Deneb are three stars in a line. They represent the swan's body and the tips of its wings. Finally, some distance away is Albireo, marking the position of the great bird's head.

Halfway along the neck of the swan is a point scientists label Cygnus X-1. If you locate Cygnus in the fall sky and gaze at the spot where Cygnus X-1 lies, you will not actually see anything. But you'll be looking at the exact point in space where scientists believe there may be a black hole.

Black holes are places where the pull of gravity is so strong that

nothing, not even light, can escape from them. Once inside a black hole, you could never come back out the same way. However, it is possible that you could escape by a different route and arrive at a totally different part of the universe. What is more, a journey into a black hole might transport you through time, either into the far future or the remote past.

Black holes may be created by the explosion of very heavy stars. A star that weighs twenty or thirty times as much as the Sun can only shine brightly for a few million years. Then it blows itself apart. During this huge explosion, known as a supernova, all the top layers of the old star are blasted away into space at high speed. However, the core of the star may remain whole.

The intense gravity of the black hole in Cygnus X-1 strips away gas from its bright companion star.

In a normal, middle-aged star, such as the sun, the core is the place where light and heat are made. The outward pressure of this light and heat prevents the inward force of gravity from squeezing the core any smaller. For most of a star's life, these two great forces struggle against one another in an evenly matched tug of war. But in a dead star, there is no longer any light pressure to oppose gravity. As a result, the core is squeezed tighter and tighter and gets smaller.

When average-size stars, such as the sun, reach the end of their lives, their cores shrink down to hot balls of squashed matter called *white dwarfs*. In bigger, heavier stars, the force of gravity acting on the dead star's core is much stronger. If the core is more than three times as heavy as the sun, nothing can prevent gravity from crushing the core. From an original size of more than 32 000 km across, the core is squashed in less than a tenth of a second to a ball only 40 km across.

At this stage, 15 mL of this matter would weigh the same as four billion full-grown elephants. But gravity squeezes the core still smaller. In a fraction of a second, it may be no larger than a period at the end of this sentence.

Within a few kilometres of the totally crushed star, gravity is so strong that it will pull in anything that comes too close. And it will allow nothing to escape, not even a ray of light. This region around the crushed star is completely black and invisible. That is why scientists call it a black hole.

If black holes are black and invisible, then how can we ever know they are there? In fact, we can't, unless there is something nearby that the black hole affects. This is the case with Cygnus X-1.

From observations made by instruments in space, scientists have discovered that huge amounts of X-rays are coming from the direction of Cygnus X-1. They have also found that a binary star lies in the same position as the source of the X-rays. A binary star consists of two stars that are circling around each other. One of the stars at Cygnus X-1 is much bigger and brighter than the sun, but its companion star is invisible. Astronomers know it is there only

because of the "wobbles" it causes in the movement of its giant neighbor.

From the extent of the wobbles, astronomers think the dark star in Cygnus X-1 must weigh from five to eight times as much as the sun. This fact alone suggests that it is likely to be a black hole. But the X-rays offer still stronger evidence. Careful studies have revealed that they are almost certainly coming from a whirlpool of extremely hot gas. This gas, scientists believe, has been stripped away from the bright, giant star by the black hole's gravitational pull.

Even before scientists found signs of real black holes, they had studied the mathematics of what black holes might be like inside. According to their theories, black holes may be the entrances to tunnels that join different regions of space and time. These strange tunnels are called *wormholes*.

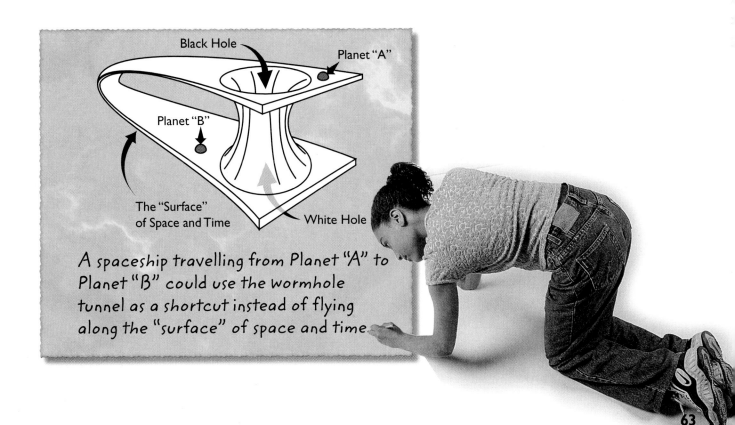

Black Hole

Planet "A"

Planet "B"

The "Surface" of Space and Time

White Hole

A spaceship travelling from Planet "A" to Planet "B" could use the wormhole tunnel as a shortcut instead of flying along the "surface" of space and time.

At the end of a wormhole is an exit known as a *white hole*. By going into a black hole, travelling along its wormhole, and then coming out the white hole at the other end, a spacecraft might be able to leap across huge distances of space and millions of years in time.

But two British scientists, Stephen Hawking and Roger Penrose, pointed out some problems with this wonderful way to travel. For one thing, there seems to be an energy barrier inside a black hole. No normal object, such as a spacecraft, could pass through this barrier without being torn to bits. Also, it appears that the wormhole tunnel would instantly squeeze shut if a piece of matter tried to move along it.

However, in 1988, new results were produced by researchers at the California Institute of Technology. These showed that a wormhole might be kept open with the help of two round plates that carried a charge of electricity. The plates would be located on either side of the "throat" leading into the wormhole.

Yet, just because something is possible in theory does not mean it will quickly, or ever, become fact. If black holes exist, then the nearest one is likely to be many trillions of kilometres away. Cygnus X-1 is about ten thousand light-years from Earth. One light-year is the distance that light travels in a year, or about 9.6 trillion km. Cygnus X-1, then, lies about 96 thousand trillion km away! At such a distance, it would be very difficult to even reach the black hole, let alone to use it as a time machine.

Scientists today do not know if black holes will ever be used as a means to jump instantly into the remote past or future. The technical problems to be overcome, even if such journeys are possible, are among the most difficult imaginable. Yet the people who lived a century ago might have thought of human missions to the moon in the same way. Where the search for black holes will lead us, no one yet knows.

ABOUT THE AUTHOR   DAVID DARLING

David Darling holds a Bachelor of Science degree in physics and a Ph.D. in astronomy. He has written more than thirty science books for young people, including *Computers of the Future: Intelligent Machines and Virtual Reality* and *The Health Revolution*. David lives in northern England with his wife and two children.

Status Extinct

by Eric Brown
Illustrated by Paul Rivoche

Jessica Ball sneezed as her ship came in to land.

She blew her nose and dropped the tissue in the waste chute. She could not believe it. Modern science had developed starships to send her to the edge of the galaxy in search of intelligent life, and yet there was still no cure for the common cold.

She sat in the darkness of the command cabin, sniffed and felt sorry for herself. She stared through the viewscreen as the ship touched down with a gentle bump. For as far as she could see, the world was covered in a thin layer of snow. Grey, leafless trees, like umbrellas stripped of their covering, dotted the hilly terrain. The sky was grey, and low on the horizon a tiny sun burned orange. Even as she watched, a new fall of snow began.

She decided to call the planet Winterworld.

"Computer," she said. "Any more information on those life forms you scanned earlier?"

She stared at the screen in front of her. Seconds later, the words appeared: LIFE FORMS TOO DISTANT FOR ACCURATE ANALYSIS: THEY ARE SMALL, SLOW MOVING, WARM-BLOODED . . . NO FURTHER INFORMATION AVAILABLE.

"Can you tell if they're intelligent?"

The reply flashed up on the screen: NO FURTHER INFORMATION AVAILABLE.

Humankind had been exploring the stars for fifty years, and not one species of intelligent alien had been found. It seemed that only humankind existed, alone in the universe. Jessica often thought that humanity was like a child growing up without playmates, lonely and in need of company.

We need to find intelligent aliens, she told herself. Humanity needs playmates.

"Computer, what's the atmosphere like out there, and the temperature?"

She read the screen. ATMOSPHERE: NINETY-EIGHT PER CENT EARTH-NORMAL, TEMPERATURE: FIVE DEGREES BELOW ZERO, ADVISE USE OF ENVIRONMENT SUIT.

"I'll do that, computer," Jessica said.

She broke her suit out of storage and climbed into it, then ran checks on the air supply and radio links. She would go out for a short exploratory walk lasting no more than thirty minutes, collecting samples of soil and plant life for computer to analyze. Later, after she had returned and slept, she would take the buggy out and explore further afield.

Before she sealed her helmet, she blew her nose for the last time. She had taken anti-influenza pills for the past twenty-four hours, but still felt no better. Her head ached and her throat was sore. She told herself that she was being weak: here she was, an intrepid pilot-explorer, complaining about a common cold.

She stepped into the airlock, and then walked down the ramp to the surface of Winterworld.

She crunched over the frost-hard ground, climbing a low hill towards a stand of bare, grey trees. Her footsteps shattered the silver leaves of a thistle-like plant that covered the surface of the land. She knelt and clumsily picked up the broken leaves in her gloved fingers, then into her samples bag.

She climbed the hill, and at the top turned to survey the view. Her orange and white ship was the only splash of color in the grey landscape. Beyond the ship to the south, a vast plain stretched away to a distant sea. She turned and looked north: the hills climbed, became foothills, then rose to become high, snow-covered mountains.

She looked down the hill, into the valley. Fifty metres away she saw a low bush decorated with yellow flowers. She decided to collect a sample of the flowers, then return to the ship.

She was half-way down the hill when she lost her footing. Her boots shot out from under her and she crashed painfully on to her back, sliding down the hillside like a runaway toboggan.

Too late, she saw the drop before her. She tried to grab hold of passing plants, tried to slow her slide. She screamed as the hillside disappeared beneath her and she fell through the air. She hit the ground with an impact that knocked the breath from her lungs, tore her suit, and smashed the face-plate of her helmet. She rolled over and over, pain shooting through her body.

She came to a stop at the bottom of the ravine. She lay on her back, staring up into the grey alien sky. When she tried to move, the pain became too much and she passed out.

She came to her senses.

The pain and the cold were too much. Her helmet was shattered, her suit torn. The cold invaded, freezing her body. She tried to move, sit up. An incredible pain shot up her right leg, making her cry out. She looked down the length of her body. Her leg below the knee was bent at an awkward angle—obviously broken.

Very well, she told herself: she must not panic. This was an emergency, but there was a way out. She would contact the ship, tell computer to send out the buggy on remote control. It would home in on her signal, locate her, and carry her back to the ship. There, she would spend some time in the healer unit and her leg would be mended. Simple.

She pulled the radio from the chest of her suit, and then stared at it in dismay. The device had been crushed in the fall and was mangled and useless.

Not to worry . . . She carried a spare radio, in case of emergencies. The trouble was—the back-up radio was in a pouch on her right boot.

As she sat up and tried to reach forward, pain shot up her leg. It was as if someone was hacking at her shin bone with an axe. She cried out, gritted her teeth, and reached out again. This time, she managed to reach her boot and pull the radio from its pouch.

Her sense of triumph lasted just five seconds.

Her fingers, numb with cold, fumbled the radio. It dropped from her grasp. She reached out for it as it slid away from her, but she was too slow. In panic she watched it skitter away over the frost-hard ground, down the ravine and out of sight.

Jessica lay back and screamed with desperation.

She tried to clear her mind, consider what to do next. She could not move. The pain from her leg was too intense. Every time she tried to drag herself up the ravine, she felt herself slipping into unconsciousness. But the simple fact was that if she failed to get back to the warmth of the ship, she would be dead in hours.

Also, she was breathing the atmosphere of this planet, and she had no idea what alien viruses might be poisoning her system. She decided that this, at the moment, was the least of her worries.

Her first priority was to get back to the ship.

She sat up, steeled herself and, using her arms to push herself up the hillside, moved about ten centimetres. Then the pain gripped her leg, and moaning in pain she passed out again.

Jessica opened her eyes.

She was so cold that she could not feel her hands and feet. She had to clamp her jaw tight shut to stop her teeth chattering. Carefully, knowing that if she passed out again she might never wake up, she tried to push herself into a sitting position.

It was impossible. She lay on her back, staring up into the sky. What a way to die, she thought; on a lonely planet five hundred light-years from Earth . . .

It was then that she thought she saw movement. Out of the corner of her eye, at the top of the ravine, she saw something move quickly, then disappear. Seconds passed by, and when nothing happened she told herself that she must have imagined the movement.

She saw it again. Something bobbed its head over the edge of the hillside and quickly looked at her, before moving out of sight. She felt a sudden stab of fear. Computer had told her that animals lived on Winterworld. What if those animals were hungry, and decided to make a meal of her?

There was more movement above her. She saw a dozen small, round heads appear over the edge of the hill. They were grey, as bald as emus' eggs, and they were staring down at her. She closed her eyes, opened them again. They were still there.

Seconds passed, and then the creatures climbed over the edge of the hill and moved down the ravine towards her, and Jessica stared in disbelief.

The creatures were not animals—but humanoids. They were tiny, perhaps a metre high and impossibly slim, their arms and legs as thin and grey as gun barrels. Jessica counted twenty of the tiny extraterrestrials. They moved slowly down the slope, as if wary of the strange creature lying at the bottom.

I don't believe it, she said to herself. Aliens—real, live humanoid aliens . . . She decided to call them Thinnies.

They approached her slowly, encircling her and moving forward. She stared at the closest being. It had a slit mouth, two holes in a flat nose, and two big, black eyes.

The aliens came within a metre of her and then crouched down on their iron-rod legs, staring at her. From time to time one would turn and speak to the others in a high, whistling voice.

Jessica raised a hand, pointing up the slope. "I . . . need your help."

At the sound of her voice, the Thinnies stood and backed off.

"The ship," she went on, pointing. "Can you get me back to my ship?"

She laughed at the uselessness of her request. They were aliens—how would they begin to understand what she was talking about?

They approached her again, settling themselves into their peculiar squats, all pointy knees and elbows, and regarded her with curiosity.

"Please," she said desperately. "Please do something to help me . . ."

The Thinnies turned and looked up the slope. Two creatures appeared on the edge of the ravine. They climbed down, dragging something after them.

It was a sledge—a crude, narrow sledge constructed from the wood of the planet's leafless trees.

They had realized what had happened to her, that she had injured herself and needed to be taken back to her ship.

The Thinnies positioned the sledge next to Jessica, and then took hold of her body and legs. She grimaced in pain and they lifted her quickly and placed her on the sledge.

She was too long for the simple vehicle, and her legs trailed on the ground. As all twenty aliens took hold of the ropes attached to the sledge and began pulling, Jessica gasped in pain as her broken leg bounced across the frozen ground.

She hovered on the edge of consciousness, the pain increasing with every passing second. They moved down the ravine, and Jessica expected the sledge to turn south and head up the hillside toward her ship.

But instead of heading toward the ship, they turned north and dragged her further into the foothills. Jessica cried out in panic. "No! You don't understand! The wrong way! Please . . . please take me back to the ship!"

They ignored her, carried her further into the hills. In the final seconds before the pain became too much and she passed out, she wondered where they were taking her, and why.

*S*he came awake slowly.

The first thing she realized was that she was no longer freezing cold. She was not exactly warm, but she could feel her hands and feet. The second thing she noticed was that she was flat on her back inside some kind of vast chamber.

She raised her head, looked around, then lay back again in disbelief. She was lying in the performance area of a big, circular amphitheatre, covered with a great membrane of material through which she could see the grey sky. The amphitheatre was full of aliens seated around the sloping banks. Perhaps thousands of the creatures were gathered there, quietly watching her.

"What do you want?" she asked weakly. "What do you want with me?"

An alien approached her, squatted, and spoke to her in its high, fluting language. Jessica shook her head. "It's no good—I don't understand you. Just as you don't understand me."

The alien stood, turned, and spoke to the gathering. It reached out a thin, stick arm to another Thinnie standing out of sight behind Jessica's head. She rolled her eyes to see what was happening, and saw one alien pass the other a long thin implement like a knife.

She closed her eyes. She could not stop herself from crying. She tried to move, to get away, but the pain from her leg, from the rest of her bruised and battered body, kept her flat on her back.

When she opened her eyes, the Thinnie was approaching her with the knife. She wondered why they were going to kill her—to provide food, as a sacrificial offering to their gods, or simply because she was a stranger who had invaded their territory?

She closed her eyes, waiting for the first blow . . .

It never came.

She felt the material of her suit being cut. Other hands pulled away the remains of her shattered helmet. When she opened her eyes she saw perhaps half a dozen Thinnies moving around her, taking away pieces of her outer suit, removing her gloves.

Two Thinnies squatted beside her and began testing her limbs with their tiny, claw-like hands. They pressed the bruised areas and touched the cuts. One alien, curious, examined the St. Christopher medallion around her neck.

They stood, spoke to the gathering.

Then they moved to her broken leg. Together, they lifted the leg and straightened the break, causing Jessica to cry out in agony. They tied her leg to something straight and cold, a splint of wood. They applied some sticky substance to her cuts and bruises, and as they busied themselves about her, Jessica closed her eyes and gave thanks that the first race of aliens discovered by humankind should prove to be so caring and—she could think of no other word for it—*humane*.

Leaving the remains of the outersuit on the ground around her, twenty of the Thinnies gathered and gently lifted her back on to the sledge, and Jessica could have wept with joy.

Lastly, the gathering of the aliens left their seats around the amphitheater and filed past where she lay, examining her with their staring black eyes, their expressions unreadable. She reached out and touched their arms, each as hard and cold as iron. She murmured, "Thank you," even though she knew that they had no way of understanding her gratitude.

Then they pulled her on the sledge from the amphitheatre, through a village of crude wooden huts, and back in the direction of her ship.

The ride was less painful this time. The splint kept her leg straight and off the ground, and the ointment they had applied to her body eased her aches and pains.

The aliens dragged the sledge up the ship's ramp and left her at the top. Jessica sat up, stared at the beings who had saved her life. She raised her hand, and the Thinnies, responding to her gesture, raised their hands also before walking down the ramp and away from the ship.

Jessica dragged herself into the airlock and through the warm ship to the surgery. She climbed into the healer, stripped off her garments, and removed the makeshift splint. She set the healer for three days, then closed the lid over her and lay back. She felt the warmth of the healer as it began its work, and slipped into a deep, peaceful sleep.

She awoke three days later, climbed from the healer, and tested her leg. It was still sore, but she could walk. She sniffed, then sneezed. The healer might have mended her broken leg, but it had done nothing to cure her cold.

She would, she realized, be famous when she returned to Earth with the news of her discovery. Her name would be known on every colony world: Jessica Ball, the first pilot-explorer to contact intelligent aliens. She imagined the vid-stations on Earth, all wanting to interview her, the crowds eager to see the woman who had met the aliens . . . In years to come there would be scientific teams sent to Winterworld to study the Thinnies and their history, to learn their language and customs.

Maybe, one day, a Thinnie might pay a visit to Earth.

But before she left Winterworld, she would return to the Thinnies and thank them, maybe take them a gift.

She took the St. Christopher's medallion from around her neck. St. Christopher, the patron saint of travellers. It would make a suitable present for the race who had helped her in her hour of need.

She climbed into her back-up suit, took the buggy from the hold, and drove from the ship. She climbed the hill and passed down the other side, moving around the ravine where she had fallen. She accelerated, speeding over the hills to the alien village.

She expected the noise of the buggy to alert them to her arrival, but if it had they did not venture from their huts to greet her. She braked, climbed from her buggy, and looked around. The place was deserted. The sun was high in the sky—it was midday. She wondered if they were in their huts, perhaps taking a meal.

She strode across to the first hut, peered inside. It was empty. She moved to the next one, and this too was deserted.

She saw the covered amphitheatre in the centre of the village. Perhaps the Thinnies were attending a meeting?

She hurried across to the amphitheatre, ducked under the skin, and walked down the slope to the central performance area where three days ago the aliens had treated her leg.

Her footsteps slowed when she saw the first aliens, and then all the others sitting and lying around the banked amphitheatre. She ran across to the nearest Thinnie, knelt, and reached out to touch the tiny being.

It sprawled on the bank, unmoving. All the others, thousands of them, lay on the bank, many clutching each other. She climbed the bank, stopping often to examine an alien she thought might still be alive.

Then she stood, stared around at the amphitheatre full of dead aliens, and a terrible thought occurred to her.

She examined the nearest Thinnie. Its eyes were inflamed, its nose-holes blocked with mucus . . .

Then Jessica saw her old suit in the centre of the performance area. Slowly, in a daze, she walked toward it, and stopped.

An alien lay next to the suit, its stick-thin arm outstretched.

Protruding from the chest of the suit, pinning it to the ground, was the long, sharp knife the alien had used three days ago to cut away her suit.

She knew what it meant, this knife in her suit. The aliens, unable to get inside the ship to kill her, had symbolically "killed" her suit . . .

For she had brought death to these innocent people; she had spread disease amongst them in the form of the influenza virus, a virus new to them and against which, therefore, they had no protection.

"I'm sorry," she whispered. "I'm so sorry."

She pulled the St. Christopher medallion from her pouch and dropped it into the hand of the dead alien.

Then, weeping, she hurried from the amphitheatre, climbed aboard the buggy, and drove at speed from the village.

Back at the ship she slumped into her seat before the viewscreen, staring out as the snow fell on Winterworld.

"Computer," she said in a small voice. "Scan for life—the life forms you detected from orbit before landing. Are there any still alive, anywhere?"

Seconds later the reply flashed across the screen: SCANNERS DETECT SMALL ANIMALS, BIRDS, NO SIGN OF ORIGINAL LIFE FORMS.

*S*he readied the ship for lift-off.

As the engines fired, she entered the computer's exploration files. She typed in the information:

Planet: WINTERWORLD

Native Fauna: HUMANOID ALIENS—INTELLIGENT

Status: . . .

Jessica hesitated, tears rolling down her cheeks.

At last she typed:

Status: EXTINCT

Then the ship lifted, carrying Jessica Ball away from Winterworld for ever.

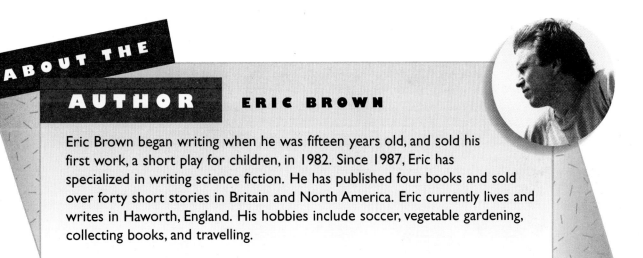

ABOUT THE AUTHOR ERIC BROWN

Eric Brown began writing when he was fifteen years old, and sold his first work, a short play for children, in 1982. Since 1987, Eric has specialized in writing science fiction. He has published four books and sold over forty short stories in Britain and North America. Eric currently lives and writes in Haworth, England. His hobbies include soccer, vegetable gardening, collecting books, and travelling.

Children of Space

Four Children, One Being.
Four Children, One Seeing.

by Julie Holder
Photographed by Gilbert Duclos

The small ship
Came down in the garden
Hardly disturbing the night.
The Being stepped out
As it landed,
Walking upright.
Its fur was like frost
In the moonshine
Sparkling with light.
It was as tall as I
No more—
It looked into my eyes
And knew me sure as sure.
I wanted to show that I liked it,
I wanted to smile—
I tried—
But it set no store
By anything I knew—
I cried . . .

No No!
The ship was huge—
The Alien too
But it had no form—
Like fog it was
You could see right through
Eyes it had, I think,
That floated round inside it
Like diamonds they were,
Faceted and prism'd
That surely denied it
Any sight as we see,
The coldness of it
Was space grown
It wasn't anything that could be known
Or could know me
It turned the color of things to grey
I was terrified—
I ran away!

Not at all!
The ship was small
But did not touch the ground.
The thing rolled out sounding laughter
And bounced around.
It shot out a sort of hand
And showed me in the palm
Stars and planets wheeling.
I thought it meant no harm
Though it whirled around and round me,
Dizzied me and sent me reeling—
I thought it was playing.
It showed me toys and treasures and keys,
Come—come with these, it said,
In no voice that I heard
But I saw that it shrank
From touching trees
And I said, without word—
I'm staying.

I was watching from the window.
What made you act so weird?
Why did you cry
And run
And stare
As though you saw something you feared?
Were you playing a game?
Or did something give you a scare?
I watched from the window
All the time—
And I saw nothing there!

E.T.

by Jean Kenward
Illustrated by Leon Zernitsky

"Extra Terrestrial" they called you, spilling
suddenly from your chariot of light,
dark
in a darkling country.
Through the bracken
your fingers fumbled.
You were never quite
with us,
but only nearly—
seemed a stranger,
yet eager to be friendly,
not to fight.

Will it be possible some day to venture
ourselves into your planet?
Leave behind
the guns, the tanks, the hatred—
carry merely
the mild, inquiring searchlights
of the mind?
Not wishing to possess
your place,
but really
prove to be simply curious,
and kind?

How the Earth Came to Be

In the days before the Earth came to be, there was just infinite space. The only things in this space were the stars. Now the stars were very far from each other. Therefore they were always lonely.

Well, this one star decided that he wanted to end his long term of loneliness, and that he had to do something about it. He thought and thought, but couldn't come up with anything. Then he discovered that, in all his thought, he had compressed a small amount of the gas with which he was made in his hand. He made more and more of these, and this is how the planets of gas were born.

After a while the star became bored with these planets, and wanted to make solid ones. As he thought and thought, something hit him in the head. It was the remains of a long-dead star. He made new planets out of the remains, and with the excess material made what we know as the asteroid belt. In one of the planets there was a deposit of oxygen and a deposit of hydrogen. There was three times more hydrogen than oxygen, so when the wall that separated the two deposits collapsed, water was formed. Eventually, life forms appeared on this planet, including humans. This planet is called Earth, and the star that made the planets is known as the sun. Thus concludes the story of how the Earth came to be.

Sheel Chaudhuri
Grade 6

> *I've always enjoyed writing ever since I was in Kindergarten. I especially like writing about space because I find it interesting and exciting!*

Sheel Chaudhuri

Life on Another Planet

I am sure many of you have heard about life on another planet. One rumor is about Martians.

In the 1800s, a scientist observed the planet Mars. To his amazement, he saw land formations like those on Earth. Immediately he claimed that there were different species on Mars. People then were very gullible, so they believed the man's theory.

In later times, reports of flying saucers were given to the government by airport officials. They were believed to have been carrying "Martians."

Now, some people think one saucer was actually a flying aircraft built by the Russians to spy on the American air force. This is quite possible, for at the time the two main powers were threatening to bomb each other.

In conclusion, I think that rumors about Martians and flying saucers are unfounded.

Aaron Haddad
Grade 6

Comet Hale-Bopp

Teachers and fellow students, today I am going to tell you about Comet Hale-Bopp.

Comet Hale-Bopp is named after the two astronomers who first discovered it in July 1995. Alan Hale of New Mexico saw it in his telescope, and Thomas Bopp of Arizona also spotted it. Comet Hale-Bopp is possibly the biggest and brightest comet to visit Earth's orbit since 1577. The most famous comet, Halley's Comet, came to visit in 1986, but it was not as bright as hoped for viewers in Canada. Just last spring we had another comet called Hyakutake. All comets come from an area just beyond the planet Neptune and travel around the sun, taking many years to return. Halley's Comet visits every 75 years. Hale-Bopp visits every 4000 years. Although Hale-Bopp may look close to us, it is really about 200 million km away, just near Mars. The sun is only 150 million km away.

A comet is made of four parts: the rocky nucleus that is followed by gas and dust that form the coma, and then the two tails, the blue gas tail and the brighter dust tail. The closer a comet gets to the sun the brighter it appears.

Believe me, if you didn't see Comet Hale-Bopp you missed something special: a truly out-of-this-world experience.

Thank you.

Jillian Davis

Age 11

I often go stargazing, and I was very excited when Comet Hale-Bopp arrived. I thought it would be the perfect subject for my speech.

Jillian Davis